COACHING
COMPASSION &
LEADERSHIP

INSIGHTS FROM BUDDHIST WISDOM

PAYAL JINDAL KHANNA

I found the Noble ... and Heart-Centered Wisdom to
deepen both my practice and conversations

Dr. Marcia Reynolds

INDIA • SINGAPORE • MALAYSIA

Dedication

Palden Gyatso

Palden Gyatso was a Tibetan Buddhist monk who endured immense suffering during his imprisonment by the Chinese government. He spent over 30 years in various labour camps and prisons, enduring torture, and starvation, and witnessing the deaths of countless fellow prisoners.

Despite the unimaginable hardships, Palden Gyatso never lost his spirit of compassion and forgiveness. In one instance, a prison guard brutally beat him, thus causing him great pain and injury. Instead of harbouring anger or seeking revenge, Palden Gyatso responded with kindness and compassion.

Years later, after his release, Palden Gyatso was asked why he did not hold any grudge or seek retribution against his captors. He replied, "If I carried hatred and anger in my heart, I would still be in prison. By forgiving and practising compassion, I set myself free."

Palden Gyatso's story serves as a powerful testament to the boundless and sweeping power of compassion—even in the face of extreme adversity. It reminds us of the capacity within each of us to choose forgiveness, understanding and love, which ultimately leads to personal liberation and the healing of our world.[1]

In loving memory of my father,
the late Shri. Bharat Bhushan Jindal,
and as an expression of profound gratitude to my mother.

Contents

Epigraph

Compassion: *Karuṇā* (Sanskrit: करुणा)

It is a significant spiritual concept in the Indic religions of Hinduism, Buddhism, Sikhism, and Jainism.

Buddhism

Karuṇā is important in all schools of Buddhism. For Theravāda Buddhists, dwelling in *karuṇā* is a means for attaining a happy present life and heavenly rebirth. For Mahāyāna Buddhists, *karuṇā* is a co-requisite for becoming a *Bodhisattva*.

Theravāda Buddhism

In Theravāda Buddhism, *karuṇā* is one of the four *divine abodes* (*brahmavihāra*), along with loving-kindness (Pāli: *mettā*), sympathetic joy (*mudita*), and equanimity (*upekkha*). In the Pāli canon, Gautama Buddha recommends cultivating these four virtuous mental states to both householders and monastics.

The Pāli commentaries distinguish between *karuṇā* and *mettā* in the following complementary manner: *Karuna* is the desire to remove harm and suffering (*ahita-dukkha-apanaya-kāmatā*) from others while *mettā* is the desire to bring about the well-being and happiness (*hita-sukha-upanaya-kāmatā*) of others.[2]

Love: *Premaḥ* (प्रेम), *anurāgaḥ* (अनुराग), *snehaḥ* (स्नेह)

Pity: *Daya* (दया)

Sympathy: *Sahanubhuti* (सहानुभूति)

Empathy: *Anukampa* (अनुकम्पा)

Altruism: *Paropakara* (परोपकार)

Love: Love in Sanskrit is known as *prema*. Love is a strong affection and care for others. It encompasses feelings of warmth, kindness, and a genuine connection to others. Love can be unconditional and is often expressed through acts of kindness and compassion—for example, the love between family members or romantic partners.

Pity: In Sanskrit, the term for pity is *daya*. Pity refers to feeling sorry for someone's suffering or misfortune. It often involves a sense of superiority or distance from the person, as it focuses on their suffering rather than their well-being. For example, feeling pity for a homeless person without taking any action to help them.

Sympathy: The Sanskrit term for sympathy is *sahanubhuti*. Sympathy is the ability to understand and share the feelings of another person. It involves feeling for someone's pain or difficulties and expressing support or concern. For example, offering condolences to a friend who has lost a loved one.

Empathy: In Sanskrit, empathy can be referred to as *anukampa*. Empathy is the capacity to deeply understand and share the emotions and experiences of another person. It involves putting oneself in another's shoes and experiencing their feelings first-hand. For example, feeling sadness or tearing up when a friend shares their personal struggle with you.

Altruism: Altruism in Sanskrit can be described as *paropakara*. Altruism refers to selfless concern for the well-being of others. It involves acting for the benefit of others without expecting anything in return. For example, volunteering at a local shelter or donating to a charitable cause.

Ethos

Giving Yourself Permission to Be Human

Foreword

Coaching Compassion and Leadership: Insights from Buddhist Wisdom offers us a fresh perspective on coaching through an Asian lens. Compassion is a key ingredient in both coaching and leadership, but sadly it is one which is neglected in both leadership development programmes and daily leadership practice. This book helps us recognise the value of compassion towards others and ourselves and amplify this trait in all our relationships particularly in coaching and to create healthier, happier and more productive workplaces.

Prof Jonathan Passmore
SVP EZRA Coaching & Henley Business School, UK

Preface

Welcome to an extraordinary journey that unfolds within the pages of this book—an expedition into the heart of compassionate living in the context of modern existence. While the themes explored here are deeply rooted in the realms of leadership, coaching, and personal development, their significance extends far beyond these arenas. This book is not just for leaders, coaches, or professionals; it is an inclusive invitation for anyone seeking to infuse their lives with purpose, empathy, and meaningful connections.

In a world often dominated by haste and material pursuits, this book underscores the vital role of compassion as the cornerstone of a meaningful life. It addresses individuals from all walks of life, recognizing that the pursuit of compassionate values and insights is not confined to a specific role or profession but is meant to resonate with your unique journey.

The relevance of this book further extends to homemakers, acknowledging the vital significance of their roles in shaping the very heart of our communities and nurturing the values that underpin our societies. Their daily routines provide a space where compassionate practices can flourish, creating a ripple effect that reaches far beyond their immediate surroundings. This book honours the essential contribution of homemakers in building this culture of compassion and offers practical tools to enhance their personal growth while tending to their responsibilities.

Throughout this book, you will encounter relatable stories, practical exercises, and thought-provoking case studies that bridge the gap between ancient wisdom and contemporary aspirations. This is not an abstract philosophical discourse; it is a guide to integrating compassion into every facet of life. The stories shared here illustrate the transformational potential that lies within each individual, waiting to be harnessed and expressed.

Whether you find yourself in a leadership role, seeking personal growth, fostering relationships, or striving for a more connected existence, this book stands as a steadfast companion on your journey. It calls attention to the void that a modern lifestyle devoid of compassion leaves and paves the way for a future where compassion forms the bedrock of leadership and coaching. The teachings explored here resonate with the essence of our interconnected world, reminding us that true fulfilment arises from meaningful connections and purpose-driven life.

This book seeks to translate compassion into action, transforming the way we lead, communicate, and live.

In the following pages, you will find a roadmap to not only discovering your own potential but also enriching the lives of those around you. Remember that this journey is not only possible- it begins here!

Prologue

In the vast setting of human existence, there are certain timeless threads that weave their way through our lives, connecting us to something greater than ourselves. Buddhism, with its deeply meaningful and impressionable teachings on compassion and mindfulness, is one such thread that has ushered and led countless individuals on a path of the mystical unravelling of the *self* where inner quiet and wisdom coalesce.

Coaching, on the other hand, represents a modern approach to the blossoming of one's being and the expansion of inherent latent potential. And in the intricate relationship between these two disciplines, a harmonious synergy emerges, creating a powerful course for a change within and collective well-being.

As a coach, I have witnessed first-hand the incredible shifts that occur when compassion becomes the driving force behind coaching relationships. I have seen individuals awaken to their brilliance, overcome their deepest fears and live lives of authenticity. And it is with great excitement and humility that I share the principles, intuitive perceptions and stories within these pages, in the optimistic expectation that they will kindle compassion within your coaching practice.

While we marvel at the remarkable intersection of Buddhism, compassion, and coaching drawing inspiration from the wisdom of the Buddha and the transformative principles of coaching, we delve into the heart of what it means to be a compassionate coach, both in our professional practice and in our own lives.

It is not just a book—it is an exploration of a paradigm shift—a shift that emphasizes the power of compassion in coaching, and its ability to create lasting positive shifts in the lives of both the coach and the client. It plunges headfirst into the core principles and methods that can elevate coaching from a mere transactional process to an ever-unfolding relational experience.

Through active listening, empathy, and skilful presence, we create a sacred space for self-exploration and self-discovery. But what happens when we infuse this coaching approach with the timeless teachings of Buddhism?

Magic!

Buddhism, at its truest, is a philosophy that presents priceless understanding and considerations into the nature of suffering and the path to liberation. It encourages us to gently tend mindfulness, compassion, and a wise discerning mind as we deal with the challenges of daily life. With the coming together of the two, we unlock a doorway to a deeper level of self-awareness, awakening the dormant seeds of compassion within us and opening our hearts to the suffering and joys of others. We will discover how our self-awareness and self-compassion play crucial roles in our ability to help those we coach.

In *Coaching Compassion & Leadership*, we see—and sometimes with a gaping mouth— how the world of Buddhism informs and enriches the coaching process. We deliberate the concepts of impermanence, non-attachment, and interconnectedness, and recognize how they can guide us in supporting our clients through life's trials and tribulations. We examine the revolutionizing power of mindfulness and meditation, discovering how they can augment our coaching presence and enable us to hold space for our clients with greater clarity, audacity and love. We attempt to hand the centre stage to the force of compassion in our coaching conversations and prepare to witness as the boundless potential of an individual unfurls before us in all its awe-inspiring splendour.

Through these pages, we will seek to add novelty to the existing coaching approaches and celebrate a new way of being—a way that is rooted in greater and ever-growing humanism. But this book is not solely about theory or abstract concepts. It is a practical guide—a playbook, if you will, designed to support seasoned and aspiring coaches to amalgamate Buddhist knowledge into their coaching practice.

This book is for the coaches who yearn to make a difference—not just in the lives of their clients but in the world at large. It is for those who recognize that the true measure of success lies not in material achievements, but in the positive impact we leave on the lives of others. It is for the coaches who believe that by cultivating compassion, we can create a ripple effect that extends far beyond the confines of a coaching session.

Dare to come along?

Then brace yourself as we traverse the uncharted depths of the human spirit and witness the miracles that unfold when Buddhist principles become the foundation of coaching.

Whether you are a seasoned coach seeking to build up your practice or someone drawn to the revolutionizing power of compassion, this book offers a pathway for blending these learnings into your own life and work. Together, let us nourish our spirit, redefine the role of the coach and together, let us unleash the immense power of compassion in creating a more compassionate world—one coaching session at a time.

May this exploration ignite a spark within you, dear reader. Let us walk hand in hand with open hearts, eager minds and a steadfast commitment to nurturing the coach's growth.

Welcome to *Coaching Compassion & Leadership*.

Leadership Reimagined—Heartfelt Connections That Serve

As we delve into the narrative, envision the coaching practice as a mirror reflecting the essence of leadership itself. In today's dynamic landscape, the role of a coach is akin to that of a leader—no longer merely orchestrating from a distance but actively engaging and guiding. This notion mirrors the prime attributes of successful leaders in the contemporary sphere. Thus, henceforth in the book, read the word and world of compassionate coaching synonymously with that of Leadership and a Leader.

In an era marked by the shift from rigid hierarchical structures to inclusive and collaborative approaches, the concept of the coach resonates powerfully with that of the leader. Compassionate coaching, infused with the wisdom of Buddhism, becomes not just a supplement but an essential facet of modern leadership.

Effective leaders understand their role to be multifaceted. They are not solely decision-makers, but rather mentors, enablers, and cultivators of untapped potential. This connection between coaching and leadership takes root as we read further into the pages of *Coaching Compassion & Leadership*.

Within this evolving paradigm, leaders find themselves embracing a new set of values. The integration of Buddhist insights and coaching techniques offers a lens through which leaders can shape environments that cherish empathy, self-awareness, and interconnectedness. These qualities, in turn, inspire teams not only to reach their goals but also to undergo profound personal and professional transformations.

As the principles of Buddhism meet the dynamic field of leadership, the concept of impermanence and non-attachment takes on fresh significance. This insight gives leaders a distinctive perspective on navigating uncertainty—a concept equally vital in both coaching and leading. Furthermore, mindfulness practices, often associated with Buddhism, become an invaluable tool for leaders. These practices foster centredness, wise decision-making, and a genuine connection with those they lead.

The fusion of compassionate coaching with leadership creates a space where relationships thrive. The compassionate leader, much like the compassionate coach, nurtures psychological safety, fosters trust, and encourages open communication—a trifecta that paves the way for innovation and collaboration. This connection resonates deeply with the coaching principle of empowering individuals to overcome self-imposed limitations and realize their untapped potential.

In a world where compassion and understanding hold unparalleled importance, the synergy between Buddhist wisdom and coaching practices is truly transformative. The book not only scaffolds efforts at personal growth but also acts as a roadmap for modern leaders seeking to truly impact their teams and organizations.

As we immerse ourselves in the exploration of the connection between compassion and coaching, let's acknowledge that this relation extends to the realm of leadership. This recognition heralds the evolution of leaders as compassionate coaches and underscores the pivotal role they play in fostering a connected and thriving world.

The Purpose, Background, and Significance of the Synergy between Buddhist Compassion and Coaching

With a loving passion for improving self and an honest reverence for the teachings of Buddhism, I have devoted this work to discerning and integrating the principles of compassion and coaching.

But why is this so significant? Throughout this book, we will uncover the unmistakable connection between these disciplines, revealing the exceptionally transformative potential they hold when combined. Drawing from the timeless wisdom of Buddhism, we will reconnoitre a bit, stepping back to awaken to the true nature of reality, mindfulness, and the cultivation of compassion. We will then nose-dive into the world of coaching, discovering practical techniques and tools to support our growth.

By intertwining these elements, we create a dance—a dance that celebrates the relationship between timeless sagacity and contemporary methodologies, between self-discovery and helping others find their paths.

Coaching Exists Because Human Desires Exist

Author's Note: A critical evaluation of the fundamental premise that coaching exists because human desires exist.

Coaching is an artful practice born out of our innermost human desires. It is a testament to our collective yearning. I encourage you to immerse yourself into what follows, shedding the inhibitions that stop us from experiencing the joys that lie around the corner and sometimes right in our laps close to our hands, and to muse and marvel at the magnificent connection between coaching and the desires that drive us.

Coaching:

It goes beyond surface-level aspirations and aims to facilitate an elemental change. It leaps into the profound, the transforming and the liberating.

By employing various coaching techniques, coaches help individuals unravel the layers of their arcane desires. The infusion of Buddhist principles imbues this process with heightened self-awareness, boundless empathy and an inner backdrop ripe for growth.

Human Desires:

In the very essence of our being, desires propel us towards progress, fulfilment and the pursuit of a meaningful existence. Psychology and neuroscience have laid bare the composite and the multifarious arras of our desires, rooted in primary human needs—autonomy, competence, relatedness, and purpose.

Coaching, with its unwavering gaze on these needs, emerges as a lighthouse, which brightens our path. It offers a tailored approach to help individuals manoeuvre the course of their desires and land a good chance at crafting a life worth aiming for.

Desires are the underlying motivations that drive individuals to seek coaching.

Coaching, for the inherent human needs it addresses, and the transformative potential it holds.

Scientific Evidence Serves as a Steadfast Ally:

Numerous studies have demonstrated the efficacy of coaching in supporting personal development and goal attainment. For example, a meta-analysis conducted by Theeboom, Beersma, and Van Vianen (2013) found that coaching interventions positively impacted individual performance, well-being, and self-regulation.[3] Another study by Grant, Curtayne, and Burton (2009) highlighted the positive effects of coaching on goal attainment and subjective well-being.[4] These findings provide empirical evidence of coaching's ability to address human desires and contribute to personal growth.

Limitations and Considerations:

While coaching does all that we discussed, it is vital to acknowledge the boundaries of coaching. Coaches are not therapists or counsellors, and they must humbly recognize when a client's needs exceed the scope of coaching. Referring clients to appropriate professionals ensures their holistic well-being and the ethical practice of coaching. Furthermore, coaches must be mindful of potential biases and cultural considerations, which inculcate diversity and inclusivity in their approach to honour the unique desires and backgrounds of their clients.

But let us not overlook the ethical responsibility that accompanies this sacred practice. Upholding the sanctity of the coaching relationship, coaches negotiate the panorama of ethical complexities with an unwavering dedication to their client's well-being, which respects their autonomy and confidentiality.

In culmination, coaching is in response to our primordial longings, an an inviting call to embrace the dormant that resides within us, thus kindling its magnificent unfolding.[5]

Chapter 1

Buddhist Compassion at the Core

In the first chapter of *Coaching Compassion & Leadership*, we lay the groundwork for understanding the essential principles that underpin compassionate coaching. We look at the core teachings of Buddhism and their relevance to the coaching process and how they form the bedrock of our coaching practice.

We begin with **The Four Noble Truths**, the foundational teachings of Buddhism. We examine the nature of suffering (*dukkha*) and its causes, highlighting how the comprehension of suffering can inform our coaching practice. We study the concept of attachment and the role it plays in our clients' lives, uncovering the ways in which attachment can hinder the advancement of self and a feeling of contentment.

The Four Noble Truths

Through insightful contemplation, we come to recognize the various forms of suffering individuals may experience in their lives, such as physical pain, emotional distress, and existential dissatisfaction. The Buddha, through his journey revolving around seeking the truth, self-discovery, and enlightenment, gained astute insights into the nature of human suffering.

One story that we will very quickly retrace from the Buddha's life which exemplifies this understanding is the story of his encounter with the **four sights**.

As a young prince, Siddhartha Gautama was sheltered from the harsh realities of life. However, one day, he ventured outside the palace walls and witnessed four sights that would forever change his path.

- The **first sight** was that of an old man, frail, and feeble. This sight highlighted the inescapable reality of ageing and the physical limitations that come with it.

- The **second sight** was that of a sick man, suffering from the ailments of the body. This sight brought to the forefront the truth of physical suffering that is inherent in human existence.

- The **third sight** was that of a funeral procession, with grieving individuals mourning the loss of a loved one. This sight exposed the painful truth of impermanence and the inevitability of death.

- Lastly, the **fourth sight** was that of a wandering ascetic, a spiritual seeker who had renounced worldly possessions and sought liberation from suffering.

These encounters strongly impacted Siddhartha, compelling him to seek answers to the fundamental human inquiries and the roots of suffering. Through his subsequent spiritual journey, he discovered **The Four Noble Truths**, which became the foundation of Buddhism.

Coaching and The Four Noble Truths

The **First Noble Truth** teaches us that suffering (*dukkha*) is inherent to life. Correctly perceiving the nature of suffering allows us, as coaches, to approach our clients with empathy, recognizing that they are dealing with their unique challenges and seeking relief from their suffering which is so very real and incomparable in degree.

The **Second Noble Truth** guides us to explore the causes of suffering (*samudya*). It reveals that attachment (taṇhā) and craving are at the root of our suffering. We become attached to desires, outcomes, identities, and even our thoughts, which can lead to dissatisfaction and discontentment. This knowledge enables us to assist our clients in diagnosing and investigating their attachments and supporting them in letting go of what no longer serves them to foster a sense of liberation.

Piloted by the wisdom of the Buddha, we look at the **Third Noble Truth**—the cessation of suffering (*nirodha*). We investigate the transformative potential of letting go, releasing attachments, and cultivating a sense of inner freedom. We discover how in the realm of coaching, attachment could manifest as limiting beliefs, self-doubt or resistance to change.

Compassionate coaching necessitates creating a nurturing space that gently guides clients toward identifying and releasing their attachments, thus inspiring them to welcome new possibilities and experience personal change.

By integrating the teachings of **The Four Noble Truths** into our coaching practice, we gain a profound twigging of the human experience and the complexities of suffering. We cultivate compassion and empathy for our clients, acknowledging their struggles and providing a safe space for inward probing and growth.

Finally, we see that within **The Fourth Noble Truth** is found the guide to the end of suffering (*magga*): **The Noble Eightfold Path**. A guide for living a life of purpose and fulfilment. We will closely study each aspect of the path, including *right understanding, right intention, right speech, right action, right livelihood, right effort, right mindfulness,* and *right concentration.* We will reflect on how these principles can support our coaching.

The Story of Kisagotami, a Disciple of Buddha:

To illustrate the power of this understanding, let us turn to a story from the Buddha's life. After attaining enlightenment, the Buddha encountered a woman named Kisagotami who was grieving the death of her only child. Consumed by sorrow, she carried her deceased child's body from house to house, desperately seeking a cure.

Upon seeing the Buddha, Kisagotami approached him and asked for a way to bring her child back to life. The Buddha, aware of her pain and the universal nature of suffering, offered her a different perspective. He told her that he could provide a solution if she could bring him a mustard seed from a household where no one had experienced death.

Eager to save her child, Kisagotami went from door to door, seeking the mustard seed. However, at each house, she encountered someone who had experienced loss and death in their lives. Through this process, Kisagotami gradually realized the universality of suffering and the fleeting nature of life.

Returning to the Buddha, Kisagotami understood the teaching he had imparted. She accepted that death is an unavoidable part of the human experience, and her attachment to bringing her child back to life was causing her immense suffering. With this newfound wisdom, Kisagotami found solace in the truth that all beings are subject to the same cycle of birth, ageing, sickness, and death.

Thus, the story of Kisagotami holds timely relevance in the context of coaching. Here is how:

1. **Impermanence and Acceptance:** The story highlights the ineluctability of change. Kisagotami's initial struggle and grief over the death of her child represent the challenges we all face when confronted with loss and change. In coaching, clients often grapple with transitions, releasing the past or accepting reality and unpleasant changes in their lives. The story of Kisagotami serves as a reminder that accepting impermanence is a vital aspect of resilience.

2. **Compassion and Empathy:** Buddha's response to Kisagotami's plea for help reflects compassion and empathy. His consideration exemplifies the coach's role in holding space for clients' emotions and experiences and allowing them to reflect on their narratives. Clients in coaching might hold narratives that are distorted or limiting. Through the coaching process, they can come to realize that the narrative they've been holding onto might not be entirely true or might not be the only perspective. This realization can lead to a new and clearer understanding of their situation, emotions, and potential solutions. Coaches can draw from this story to support clients through difficult situations.

3. **Challenging Perspectives and Limiting Beliefs**: The story invites us to examine our perspectives and beliefs. Kisagotami's desperate search for a mustard seed from a death-free household reveals her attachment to the notion that her situation is unique and unbearable. This concept resonates in coaching, where clients may perceive their challenges as insurmountable and might face a similar sense of hopelessness. Coaches can aid clients in challenging this perspective, broadening their awareness, and discovering fresh solutions.

4. **Self-awareness**: The story emphasizes the power of self-awareness. Kisagotami's encounter with Buddha awakened her to the realities of life and the absoluteness of suffering. Buddha's instruction for Kisagotami to find a mustard seed from a household untouched by death was a contemplative task. This guided reflection encouraged her to engage her awareness in exploring the Universal Truth.

   In coaching, cultivating self-awareness enables clients to scrutinise their thoughts, emotions and patterns, leading to greater clarity.

5. **Letting Go and Moving Forward**: Kisagotami's journey towards acceptance and enlightenment symbolizes the process of letting go and moving forward. The story of Kisagotami can inspire clients to reflect on areas of their lives where they might be clinging to things that no longer benefit them and create a vision for their future.

Similarly, coaches can partner with the clients in shifting their focus from seeking to control external circumstances to cultivating inner resilience.

Corporate Culture: The Four Noble Truths in Coaching

Let us see how **The Four Noble Truths** can be applied to draw parallels with a modern corporate setup.

1. **The Truth of Suffering**: In a corporate setting, suffering can manifest as stress, burnout, conflicts or a lack of fulfilment. A coach can help

clients spot and acknowledge their sources of suffering, such as unrealistic expectations, work-life imbalance or unfulfilling roles. Through introspection, clients can gain awareness of their challenges and their impact on well-being.

2. **Truth of the Cause of Suffering**: The cause of suffering, according to Buddhism, is attachment and craving. In a corporate setting, this can manifest as an obsession with material gains, power or external validation, toxic work environments, excessive pressure, or a lack of alignment with personal values. A coach can support clients in getting to the root causes of their suffering, probing factors such as ineffective communication, limited autonomy, or a mismatch between values and organizational culture.

    This can lead to a shift in focus towards more meaningful values and purposes and a healthier and more fulfilling work environment.

3. **Truth of the Cessation of Suffering**: This truth emphasizes that suffering can be overcome by letting go of attachments and desires. In a modern corporate setup, this can translate into cultivating a culture that promotes work-life balance, mindfulness practices, and fostering a sense of purpose beyond financial success. Clients can work with a coach to develop strategies for alleviating suffering. This may involve setting boundaries, polishing resilience, developing effective coping mechanisms, or recceing opportunities for growth and career development.

4. **Truth of the Path to the Cessation of Suffering**: This truth highlights the importance of following a path or a set of practices to alleviate suffering. In a corporate context, this can involve fostering a culture of open communication, empathy, and collaboration.

A coach can help clients clarify values, set meaningful goals, enhance communication skills, foster positive relationships, or explore alternative career paths. The coach can provide support as clients take steps to create a more satisfying work environment.

A coach can therefore support clients in integrating **The Four Noble Truths** by:

- facilitating self-reflection and awareness of sources of suffering in the client's unique context

- assisting in identifying and challenging limiting beliefs or behaviours that contribute to suffering

- guiding clients in exploring strategies to create a healthier work-life balance and experience well-being

- helping clients develop resilience, coping mechanisms, and self-care practices to deal with challenges

- supporting clients in aligning their values and goals with their work and finding purpose and fulfilment

Conclusion:

In this opening chapter, we've laid the groundwork for compassionate coaching by diving into the foundational principles of Buddhism. Through the study of **The Four Noble Truths** and the concept of attachment, we've begun the journey to understanding how these ancient teachings can deeply enrich and guide our coaching practice.

In the subsequent chapters, we will continue to discern the richness of Buddhism and its immaculate integration with coaching.

By synthesising these profound teachings and our coaching practice, we create a powerful framework for improving the quality of our lives.

The root of suffering is attachment.

– Buddha

Chapter 2

Heart-Centred Wisdom

A Zen story that reflects the power of compassion and presence in Buddhism:

Once, a renowned Zen master named Hakuin was approached by a samurai warrior. The samurai, known for his fierce temperament, demanded that Hakuin explain the concepts of heaven and hell.

Hakuin looked at the samurai and replied, "You impudent fool! You dare to ask such a profound question while standing before me? You are nothing but a dirty ronin!"

The master's words and tone were filled with contempt.

Enraged, the samurai drew his sword and raised it as he was ready to strike Hakuin down. But before he could make a move, Hakuin calmly spoke, "This is hell."

The samurai paused, struck by Hakuin's presence and response. At that moment, the anger and aggression in the samurai dissipated, and he sheathed his sword. Humbled, he lowered his head and thanked Hakuin for the teaching.

Hakuin then gently said, "And this is heaven."

The story illustrates how Hakuin's mindfully compassionate response transformed the samurai. By meeting aggression with calmness and insight, Hakuin guided the samurai to a realization of the destructive nature of his anger. Through this encounter, the samurai discovered the possibility of finding heaven within the depths of his being and the power of presence and compassion.

In a world where stress, reactivity, and self-doubt can easily overshadow our true potential, there exists a powerful force that has the capacity to heal, inspire, and change lives. This force is none other than compassion—a quality that runs within each and every one of us, waiting to be awakened and harnessed. Building upon the understanding of Buddhism from Chapter 1, Chapter 2 focuses specifically on the concept of compassion (*karuna*) in Buddhism. We explore how compassion is not merely a sentimental feeling but a genuine desire to ease suffering for all. We peek into the practice of loving-kindness (*metta*) meditation and how it helps cultivate compassion towards oneself and others.

We also discuss the Buddhist teachings on the bodhisattva ideal which inspires individuals to embody compassion and take a step forward and engage in compassionate action in the world.

Key Themes and Insights:

Compassion and its Multifaceted Nature:

In the context of Buddhism, compassion extends beyond conventional notions of sympathy and empathy. It stems from a clear grip on the fact that we are all linked.

In today's world, where global issues affect us all, understanding our interconnected nature is essential for creating sustainable solutions. Coaches who grasp this principle bring a holistic perspective to their practice, thus recognizing that the well-being of one individual is intricately tied to the well-being of the collective. By cultivating this awareness, coaches can guide their clients towards compassionate action that not only benefits themselves but also contributes to the greater good of humanity.

Imagine a massive puzzle, where each piece represents a person on this planet. Now, think about how when each piece fits right, the whole picture becomes clearer and more beautiful. Just like that, our world is like an intricate puzzle, where we all matter. If your piece is happier, healthier, and more fulfilled, it makes the whole picture better. So, when a coach helps the client see this connection, they're not just making their life better; they're making the entire puzzle of humanity more vibrant and complete. Our well-being ripples out, making a positive impact that touches lives beyond our own. And that's why understanding this connection matters—because our happiness isn't just about us; it's about all of us fitting together in a better world.

This chapter invites coaches to study this very essence of compassion in a practical and meaningful way.

And this is how we can do that:

1. **Cultivating Loving-kindness:** The practice of loving-kindness (*metta*) meditation is revealed here as a potent tool for cultivating compassion. Coaches should incorporate this into their personal practice to foster a sense of goodwill and compassion towards themselves and others. This practice helps coaches develop an authentic and caring disposition that can be channelled into their coaching relationships.

2. **Self-compassion:** Coaches are to cultivate self-compassion which is a pivotal cornerstone for extending compassion to their clients. By nurturing a compassionate relationship with oneself, coaches can model and facilitate self-compassion in their clients.

3. **The Bodhisattva Ideal:** The concept of the bodhisattva—an individual who aspires to attain enlightenment or absolute happiness in contemporary terms for the benefit of all beings—is studied here. Coaches are invited to embody the spirit of the bodhisattva by manifesting their inner altruism.

   The idea of embodying the bodhisattva ideal might seem unreal or unnecessary to some of us but it's like upgrading the coaching approach from regular to remarkable. It's about going beyond just the technical skills of coaching. It's adding that special ingredient.

   Think of coaching as a toolkit for growth and success. Now, consider adding an extra tool—the bodhisattva mindset. This tool isn't about wearing a superhero cape. It's about bringing an extra layer of purpose and impact to your coaching. The bodhisattva ideal isn't about being a do-gooder just for the sake of it. It's about amplifying the impact of coaching sessions.

Logical thinkers can see this as a smart move. It's not just about helping clients achieve goals; it's about helping them become catalysts for positive change in their surroundings. So, while it might sound a bit idealistic at first, it's like giving your coaching practice a heart and that heart is what can truly make a difference, not only in the lives of clients but in the world at large.

4. **Compassionate Listening**: The chapter emphasizes the importance of compassionate listening in the coaching relationship. Coaches can learn to listen for more—not only to the words spoken by their clients but also to the emotions, body language and unspoken messages. By cultivating compassionate listening skills, coaches create a space for clients to share their experiences and feel truly heard and understood.

This chapter underscores that compassion in Buddhism goes beyond mere intention—it manifests in **compassionate action**. Coaches are encouraged to support their clients in translating insights gained from coaching sessions into practical actions that can herald change.

Key Practices:

1. **Compassionate Self-Reflection**: Coaches are encouraged to engage in self-reflection and introspection to bolster their understanding of compassion and its role in their coaching practice. They must look within at their own beliefs, attitudes and behaviours to ensure that there is an alignment with the principles of compassion.

2. **Skilful Questioning**: Coaches are urged to employ *skilful questioning* techniques that prompt clients to probe their suffering and develop insights. By asking open-ended questions which bring about reflection, coaches can partner with the clients in finding their solutions.

Here are some examples that illustrate the concepts discussed:

1. Loving-kindness Meditation:

Coaches start each day with a loving-kindness meditation practice. They visualize their clients and send wishes of well-being, happiness, and peace towards them. This practice helps the coach cultivate a genuine caring attitude and develop a sense of compassion for their clients.

Let's consider a study conducted by Barbara L. Fredrickson, a leading researcher in the field of positive psychology, in which participants were asked to practice loving-kindness meditation, similar to what coaches can do.[6] The results showed that participants who engaged in this meditation practice experienced an increase in positive emotions, such as joy, gratitude, and love.

This suggests that the act of sending positive wishes and goodwill towards others through meditation can actually create a positive shift in our emotional state. When coaches begin their day with a loving-kindness meditation, they're setting a positive tone for themselves which can naturally translate into a more empathetic and effective coaching approach, benefitting both coaches and their clients.

So, while it might sound simple, there's scientific evidence to support this practice.

Loving-Kindness Meditation Practice Steps:

1. Find a quiet and comfortable space where you can relax without interruptions.

2. Take a few deep breaths to centre yourself and bring your attention to the present moment.

3. Close your eyes and bring a person in your life to mind—someone whom you care about or feel neutral towards. It can be someone close to you, a client, a friend, a colleague, or even a stranger you have recently encountered.

4. Visualize this person in your mind and imagine their presence before you.

5. As you hold this image of the person in your mind, start repeating the following phrases silently or out loud while adapting them to the person you have visualized:

    ◆   "May you be happy."

    ◆   "May you be healthy."

    ◆   "May you be safe."

    ◆   "May you live with ease."

6. As you repeat each phrase, try to genuinely connect with the intention of sending wishes of well-being, happiness, and peace towards this person. Allow your words to carry a sense of love, compassion, and genuine goodwill.

7. If your mind wanders or distractions arise, gently bring your attention back to the person and the phrases. Do not force anything. Simply allow yourself to be present with the practice.

8. After a few minutes of offering loving-kindness to this person, gradually expand your focus to include yourself. Visualize yourself in your mind's eye, and repeat the same phrases, directing them towards yourself:

    ◆   "May I be happy."

    ◆   "May I be healthy."

    ◆   "May I be safe."

    ◆   "May I live with ease."

9. As you offer these wishes of well-being to yourself, allow yourself to receive them fully and feel a sense of kindness and compassion towards yourself.

10. Finally, if you feel ready, you can expand the practice further to include other people in your life—loved ones, acquaintances or even challenging

individuals. Visualize each person in your mind and offer the same phrases of loving-kindness towards them.

11. Take a few moments to sit in silence and allow the energy of loving-kindness to permeate your being and radiate outwards.

12. When you are ready, gently open your eyes and take a few moments to reflect on your experience. Notice any shifts in your emotions, thoughts or sensations.

This loving-kindness meditation practice allows you to develop a sense of connection, empathy, and well-wishing. Regular practice can strengthen your capacity for compassion, thus positively influencing your relationships and overall well-being.

Clients can be inspired to practice for similar reasons.

2. Self-Compassion:

During a coaching session, a client expresses feelings of self-doubt and criticism. The coach recognizes the opportunity to introduce the concept of self-compassion. They guide the client through an exercise where they practice by offering themselves acceptance, kindness, love, and forgiveness.

Exercise Cultivating Self-kindness

Objective:

The purpose of this exercise is to support clients in nurturing a compassionate relationship with themselves. By practising it, clients can shift their self-talk and develop a more loving and supportive internal dialogue, which leads to holistic well-being.

Instructions:

1. Find a quiet and comfortable space where you can relax without interruptions.

2. Take a few deep breaths to centre yourself and bring your attention to the present moment.

3. Close your eyes and bring to mind a recent situation where you felt self-critical or experienced self-doubt. Visualize yourself in that situation.

4. Reflect on the thoughts and words you directed towards yourself during that situation. Notice the tone and language you used.

5. Now, imagine that a dear friend or loved one is experiencing the same situation and feeling the way you did. Visualize this person in your mind.

6. Begin to shift your perspective and imagine what you would say to your friend or loved one in that situation. What words of kindness, consideration and support would you offer them? Consider how you would encourage and uplift them.

7. Now, imagine redirecting those same kind and supportive words towards yourself. Visualize yourself as the recipient of your compassion.

8. Repeat the following phrases silently or out loud, adapting them to your specific situation:

    - "I am deserving of kindness and understanding."

    - "I acknowledge my efforts and progress."

    - "I embrace myself with love and acceptance."

    - "I am resilient, and I can learn and grow from this experience."

    - "I am enough just as I am."

9. Allow yourself to feel the warmth and gentleness of these words as you repeat them in your heart.

10. Take a few moments to reflect on the experience. Notice any shifts in your emotions, thoughts, or physical sensations.

11. Whenever you catch yourself engaging in self-criticism or self-doubt, bring the phrases and feelings of self-kindness from this exercise to mind. Use them as a reminder to treat yourself with the love that you deserve.

12. Practice this exercise regularly, particularly during moments of self-criticism or when you feel the need for self-compassion. Over time, you will strengthen your ability to offer yourself kindness and support.

Regular practice can empower clients to have a compassionate relationship with themselves.

3. The Bodhisattva Ideal:

Coaches and their clients survey the concept of the bodhisattva ideal, where the client expresses a desire to make a positive impact in their communities. Coaches support clients in ascertaining their unique skills and passions, thus helping them develop a plan to contribute their talents towards a cause that they sincerely care about. This process catalyzes the clients' sense of honest concern and inspires them to engage in compassionate action.

The story of Ksitigarbha, also known as Ksitigarbha Bodhisattva, holds relevance in the modern context of life coaching in several ways. Ksitigarbha is revered in Buddhism as a compassionate bodhisattva or monk who vows to alleviate the suffering of beings and not to achieve Buddhahood and guide all living beings until all hells are emptied.[7]

His story offers valuable insights and lessons that can inform and inspire life coaches in their work with clients.

1. **Compassionate Service**: Ksitigarbha's vow to help beings in the realms of hell resonates powerfully in modern life-coaching. This story reminds coaches to accompany clients on their journey, acknowledge their pain and empower them to heal and thrive, especially during challenging times when clients may be experiencing their *hells* of suffering. It emphasizes the role of coaches as compassionate

companions. Its message of compassion speaks to the core principles of effective coaching today.

2. **Holding Space**: Ksitigarbha's willingness to enter the realms of hell demonstrates the importance of holding space for clients in their darkest moments. Life coaches can learn from this story to establish an environment of trust and acceptance where clients can express their struggles, dreams, and vulnerabilities openly, knowing that they will be met with love and unconditional positive regard.

3. **Transformation and Redemption**: Ksitigarbha's dedication to helping beings in hell implies a belief in transformation and redemption. Similarly, life coaches can hold belief in the potential of their clients for continual development and constructive transformation. The story encourages coaches to adopt a strength-based approach, thus focusing on the client's inherent capacity for reformation, resilience, and personal progress.

4. **Deep Listening and Empathy**: Ksitigarbha's commitment to comprehending the suffering of beings in hell underscores the importance of engaged listening and steadfast concern even when the context seems dark and difficult. In a modern setting, it denotes unconditional presence and an ability to attune to clients' needs and experiences without disturbing interferences. Life coaches can emulate this quality by seeking to understand and empathize with clients' experiences. Coaches can thereby build remarkable trust, connection, and rapport with their clients.

5. **Transcending Limiting Beliefs**: Ksitigarbha's story embodies the idea of breaking self-imposed limitations or the notion that certain challenges are insuperable. The story of Ksitigarbha defies the notion that our actions have limited impact or that our efforts are insufficient to support ourselves and others. It serves as a reminder that each individual has the potential to make a meaningful difference in the

world and contribute to the welfare of others. It imparts the message of discovering a larger purpose in the greater scheme of things. Life coaches can stimulate clients to contest confining ideas, paralysing fears and doubts that are usually born of one's mind and are largely untrue. The story inspires coaches to steer clients in unearthing their values, passions and aspirations beyond their perceived constraints.

Overall, the narrative of Ksitigarbha provides a poignant reflection on the stoic influence of compassion and service. It serves as a source of enduring inspiration for life coaches to embody these qualities in their work, thus adeptly assisting clients in traversing the struggles, discovering their inner reservoirs of strength and progressing towards a life imbued with contentment.

Examples of questions to nurse this ***beingness***:

1. What does 'make a positive impact' in your community mean to you? How do you envision this impact manifesting?

2. How does the concept of the bodhisattva ideal resonate with your desire to make a positive difference? In what ways do you connect with the idea of compassionately serving others?

3. Are there specific areas or causes in your community that you feel drawn to support or contribute to? What motivates you to engage with these areas?

4. What strengths, skills or resources do you possess that could be utilized in making a positive impact? How can you leverage these assets to serve others effectively?

5. What potential challenges or obstacles do you anticipate in your journey to make a positive impact? How can you manage these challenges and stay committed to your aspirations?

6. How do you define success in terms of making a positive impact? What markers or indicators would you use to measure your progress or effectiveness?

7. In what ways can you integrate the principles of compassion, empathy, and mindfulness into your efforts to make a positive impact? How might these qualities enhance your ability to connect with others and address community needs?

8. How can you ensure self-care and balance while dedicating yourself to serving others? How will you prioritize your well-being to sustain your commitment in the long run?

9. Who can you turn to for support, guidance, or collaboration in your journey to make a positive impact? Are there individuals or organizations that share similar values and goals?

10. What steps or actions can you take right now to begin your journey towards making a positive impact in your community? How can you start small and build momentum over time?

These questions help the client to look at their aspirations, motivations, and practical considerations related to making a dent in the world. They initiate self-reflection, goal-setting, and the integration of compassionate principles into their efforts. Through this, the client develops actionable plans with clarity and brings into line their intentions with the bodhisattva ideal, which furthers a purposeful engagement with their community.

4. Compassionate Listening:

During a coaching session, a client shares a story of a confounding experience that they went through. The coach listens without interruption. The coach responds with love and validation so that the client feels heard and understood. This compassionate listening cultivates trust and facilitates the client's consideration of their travails and potential solutions.

Examples:

1. ***Client***: *"I feel so frustrated with my progress. It seems like everyone else is advancing in their careers, but I'm stuck."*

    Coach: *"It's completely understandable to feel frustrated when it seems like others are moving ahead while you feel stuck. It can be challenging to see others' progress when you're not where you want to be. I want you to know that your feelings are valid, and we can work together to discuss strategies to help you move forward."*

2. ***Client***: *"I made a mistake in that project, and I can't stop beating myself up over it. I feel like such a failure."*

    Coach: *"Mistakes happen to everyone, and it's natural to feel disappointed or frustrated with ourselves when they occur. Remember that making mistakes doesn't define your worth or competence. It takes courage to acknowledge and learn from them. Let's see how you can use this experience as an opportunity for personal evolution and advancement."*

3. ***Client***: *"I've been feeling overwhelmed lately, trying to balance work and personal life. I'm constantly pulled in different directions."*

    Coach: *"It sounds like you have a lot on your plate and finding balance can be quite challenging. It's common to feel overwhelmed when juggling multiple responsibilities. Your emotions matter, and I want you to understand that. Let's collaborate to look at fresh and inventive ways to create more balance and self-care in your life."*

4. ***Client***: *"I had a disagreement with my friend, and now I'm questioning the entire friendship. I feel so hurt and betrayed."*

    Coach: *"Experiencing a disagreement with a friend can be really tough, especially when it affects the trust and closeness in the relationship. Your feelings of hurt and betrayal are completely rational. It is important to give yourself time and space to process these emotions. We can also probe ways to communicate and work through the situation if that feels right for you."*

5. ***Client***: *"I've been trying so hard to change my habits, but it feels like I keep slipping back into old patterns. I'm disappointed in myself."*

Coach: *"Changing habits can be a gradual and sometimes challenging process. It's completely normal to have setbacks along the way. Instead of being too hard on yourself, let's acknowledge the effort you're putting in and the progress you've already made. Remember that setbacks are part of the journey, and we can get on with looking at effective strategies to achieve our goals."*

5. Skilful Questioning:

A coach engages in skilful questioning to help clients uncover their relationship with difficult colleagues at work. Instead of asking leading or judgemental questions, the coach asks open-ended questions that encourage the client to reflect on their feelings, needs and perceptions. These skilful questions support the client in gaining insights into their patterns and developing compassionate perspectives towards the colleague which allow them to reframe the situation, bringing about resolution.

Examples:

1. What do you think might be the underlying needs or concerns for both you and your colleague in this relationship?

   This question prompts the client to consider the innermost needs and motivations that may be driving their actions and those of their colleague. This is to generate resonance and a better comprehension of both perspectives.

2. How do you typically respond when you encounter challenges or conflicts with others in the workplace and what is the impact?

   This question helps the client unearth their patterns of behaviour, responses and their impact in difficult situations, encouraging self-reflection and self-awareness.

3. Can you envision a different way of approaching the relationship with your colleague that would align with your values as well as a heightened sense of compassion?

This question invites the client to think of alternative ways of interacting with their colleague that prioritize compassion and understanding leading to a resolution in the relationship.

These instances beautifully showcase how compassion, a core principle in Buddhism, can seamlessly merge into the coaching process, leading to remarkable metamorphosis for both coaches and clients. This powerful convergence becomes a catalyst for self-realization and meaningful shifts within the coaching journey.

Here is a case study that further exemplifies the application of compassion in coaching:

Case Study: Cultivating Self-compassion

Client: Maria

Background: Maria is a high-achieving professional who constantly pushes herself to meet ambitious goals. She often criticizes herself harshly when she falls short, thus leading to feelings of self-doubt and burnout. She seeks coaching to find ways to manage her self-criticism.

Coaching Approach:

The coach recognizes the importance of cultivating self-compassion as a foundation for Maria's wish and integrates the principles of compassion (as elaborated in this chapter) by implementing specific strategies to support Maria.

Coaching Process:

1. **Establishing Trust and Connection:**

   The coach establishes a secure and impartial environment where Maria feels at ease sharing her insecurities and vulnerabilities. Building a strong coaching relationship rooted in faith in the process and the person is essential for Maria's willingness to explore her self-critical tendencies.

2. **Raising Awareness:**

   The coach helps Maria develop an awareness of her self-critical thoughts and the negative impact they have on her well-being. Through insight-generating statements, questions, and reflection exercises, the coach supports Maria in recognizing the patterns of self-criticism and the associated emotions and behaviours.

3. **Introducing Self-Compassion:**

   The coach introduces the concept of self-compassion and explains how it can positively influence Maria's self-perception and overall well-being. The professional discusses the three elements of self-compassion—self-kindness, humanity, and mindfulness.

4. **Self-compassion Practices:**

   The coach guides Maria through self-compassion practices, including self-compassionate writing exercises and guided meditations. These practices help Maria develop a compassionate and supportive internal dialogue, thus challenging her self-critical beliefs and enabling self-acceptance.

5. **Mindfulness and Self-reflection:**

   The coach encourages Maria to practice mindfulness exercises, such as mindful breathing and body scans to cultivate present-moment awareness and observe her self-critical thoughts without judgement. Through self-reflection exercises, Maria explores the underlying fears and insecurities that drive her self-criticism.

6. **Integration and Action Steps:**

The coach collaborates with Maria to identify practical steps, which she can take to integrate self-compassion into her daily life. They develop an action plan that includes setting realistic expectations, celebrating accomplishments, and engaging in self-care activities that nourish self-love.

Results and Impact:

Over the course of multiple coaching sessions, Maria witnesses substantial shifts in her mindset and emotional well-being. She becomes more attuned to her tendencies for self-judgement and learns to respond to herself with gentleness and empathy. Maria starts to value her efforts and triumphs, even when they do not meet her high expectations. Consequently, she experiences decreased stress, improved self-assurance, and an overall sense of fulfilment in life.

Through the compassionate coaching approach, Maria develops self-compassion as a potent instrument for phenomenal shifts in her mindset. This case study validates how compassionate coaching can propel individuals to water the seed of self-love, thus catalysing favourable changes within their personal spheres.

Conclusion:

In Chapter 2, we've grasped the essence of compassion in Buddhism. It's not just a sentiment; it's the genuine desire to alleviate suffering for all beings. Through loving-kindness meditation and the bodhisattva ideal, we've studied ways to cultivate and embody compassion. As we move forward, let's carry this understanding into our coaching journey, where compassion becomes the mainstay of transformative change.

The way is not in the sky. The way is in the heart.

– Buddha

Chapter 3

The Coaching Compass

Here is a story often shared by Timothy Gallwey, the author of **The Inner Game** series, to explain coaching:

Once, Gallwey was approached by a man who wanted to improve his tennis game. The man expressed his frustration and mentioned that he often struggled with making errors during matches. Gallwey agreed to help him and began observing him play. During their first practice session, Gallwey noticed that the man had a habit of tensing up right before hitting the ball. This tension seemed to be the root cause of his errors. Gallwey decided to try a different approach.

He asked the man to imagine that he had a small fish in his hand and instructed him to toss it gently into the air. As the man attempted to mimic the action, his movements became fluid and relaxed. Gallwey then told him to imagine that the tennis ball was the fish and to hit it with the same ease and naturalness. To their surprise, the man's shots became smoother, more accurate, and effortless. By shifting his focus from the outcome of the shot to the quality of his movements, he was able to bypass his self-judgement and access a state of flow.

This story illustrates the essence of coaching according to Timothy Gallwey. It emphasizes the importance of shifting the focus from external results to the process itself. By providing guidance, feedback, and alternative perspectives, a coach can help individuals tap into their inner resources, discover their solutions and unleash their full potential.[8]

In Chapter 3, we delineate the tenets of coaching, outlining its origins, principles, and core competencies. We explore the role of the coach as a facilitator of change, partnering with clients in clarifying their goals, overcoming stories from the past, and maximising their potential. We discuss the importance of establishing a coaching relationship built on trust, confidentiality, and mutual respect through examples. We also introduce the core coaching skills, such as powerful questioning, active listening, and goal setting that form the basis of an effective coaching practice.

The Origins of Coaching:

To understand the essentials of coaching, it is essential to go back to its probable origins. Coaching has evolved from diverse fields, each contributing unique perspectives and techniques. Psychology, with its focus on human behaviour and growth, provided the foundation for understanding the mind and emotions. Management theory brought concepts of leadership, motivation, and goal setting. Sports coaching emphasized performance, skill development, and achievement. By integrating these disciplines, coaching emerged as a holistic approach that addresses various aspects of personal and professional life.

A Divergent Approach

Folklore and Giants: Greek Mythology

The origins of coaching can be traced back to various ancient civilizations, including Greek mythology, which tells tales that echo the essence of coaching principles and practices. Let us explore some mythological figures and stories that may feature the origins of coaching in Greek mythology.

a) **Prometheus**, the legendary figure from Greek mythology, assumed the role of a benefactor, imparting invaluable gifts to humanity. Through his act of stealing fire from the gods and gifting it to humans, he symbolized the transmission of knowledge, enlightenment, and guidance.

   Within the domain of coaching, a parallel dynamic emerges. Coaches, akin to Prometheus, act as stimuli for change and progress. While they do not directly bestow gifts/civilization upon their clients, they spark ingenuity that affects the individual's evolution much like what fire did to the course of evolution. By partnering with clients to manifest their inner resources, coaches do much the same.

Prometheus's defiance of the gods serves as a metaphor for challenging societal limitations and adopting a growth mindset. Coaches inspire their clients to break free from self-imposed boundaries, thus cheering them to consider new horizons and strive for excellence.

Coaches, like Prometheus, are driven by a deep commitment to the betterment of humanity. They champion the advancement of individuals, nurture their strengths to help them harness their inner fire, celebrate their unique talents and chart out a new course for themselves that they aspire for.

In this parallel, Prometheus epitomizes the essence of coaching—an emblem of inspiration, empowerment, and transformation, which guides humanity towards its fullest potential.[9]

b) **Chiron,** the wise centaur of Greek mythology, serves as a classic example of a coach or mentor. Known as the wisest and most just of the centaurs, he is often depicted with the upper body of a human and the lower body of a horse. Unlike other centaurs, Chiron was renowned for his healing abilities. Like a skilled mentor, Chiron imparted wisdom, knowledge, and skills to his protégés, thus enabling them to reach their highest potential. He guided heroes, such as Achilles and Jason in various domains, including archery, medicine, and philosophy, much like a coach who supports individuals in polishing their overall strengths and capabilities.

Despite his wisdom and kindness, Chiron experienced great personal suffering. In a tragic incident, he was accidentally wounded by a poisoned arrow fired by Heracles (Hercules). Although Chiron was immortal, he could not heal himself from the wound. In a selfless act, Chiron traded his immortality with Prometheus, the Titan who had been punished by Zeus for stealing fire from the gods. As a result, Chiron was released from his suffering and allowed to die, while Prometheus gained his freedom.

Chiron's story is a prime example of a wounded healer, which symbolizes the ability to bring healing to others despite personal pain. His selflessness makes him an enduring figure in Greek mythology, and he is often revered as a symbol of inner healing and growth.

This parallel between Chiron and coaching or mentoring stands justified as it spotlights the role, which a mentor or a coach can play in directing the lives of their clients towards personal markers of success. The reference to Chiron's teachings and mentorship can be found in various Greek mythological texts, such as Homer's *Iliad* and Apollonius of Rhodes' *Argonautica*, which recount the stories of Achilles and Jason under Chiron's guidance.[10]

c) **Socrates:** While not a mythological figure, Socrates, a philosopher from ancient Greece, played a significant role in the development of coaching principles. Socrates' *Socratic Method*, characterized by probing questions and critical thinking, aimed to facilitate self-reflection, introspection, and the discovery of one's truth. His approach laid the foundation for the coaching practice of powerful questioning and guiding individuals to find their answers.[11]

d) **Orpheus:** Orpheus was a legendary musician, poet, and storyteller. His ability to enchant others with his music and poetry reflects the power of storytelling and its role in coaching.

The art of storytelling in coaching shares a profound connection with Orpheus's ability to captivate and inspire. Just as Orpheus used his music and poetry to touch the hearts and minds of his listeners, coaches can harness the power of storytelling to engage and enthuse their clients. By narrating histories and accounts, or using metaphors that resonate with their clients' experiences and aspirations, coaches can create a powerful vehicle for lasting changes.

Drawing from the mythological references, coaches can closely ponder the symbolism of Orpheus' journey to the underworld to retrieve his beloved, Eurydice. This can serve as a metaphor for the courageous self-search of one's inner depths and the willingness to face and overcome hardships, in manoeuvring personal underworlds and emerging stronger, wiser and more resilient.

The parallels between Orpheus' artistry and coaching further extend beyond storytelling. Just as Orpheus used his music to harmonize and bring unity, coaches can help individuals integrate different aspects of their lives and align them with their values and aspirations in creating desired and balanced lives.[12]

It is important to note that while all the above are mythological figures, the archetypal lessons embedded in the stories resonate with universal themes of self-reformation and introspection. While there may not be specific academic references directly linking the approaches to coaching, studying the mythological narratives and their relevance to human psychology and development can bring rich insights for coaches and their clients, and provide a broader perspective on life and sometimes its daunting facets.

In addition to Greek mythology, another ancient tale that provides a parallel to the origins of coaching is the *Epic of Gilgamesh*. Dating back to ancient Mesopotamia, the story of Gilgamesh presents valuable peeks into the human quest for meaning, connection, and self-actualisation. It is one of the oldest known works of literature.

Gilgamesh: The protagonist of the epic, is a powerful and arrogant king who sets out on a journey to seek immortality after the death of his friend, Enkidu. Along his pursuit, Gilgamesh encounters numerous roadblocks and obstacles including battles with mythical creatures and encounters with gods that ultimately lead him to confront his mortality and the limitations of his power. Finally, Gilgamesh realizes the futility of his quest for immortality and learns to appreciate the value of living a meaningful life and leaving a lasting legacy.

The epic looks at themes of friendship, mortality and the search for purpose and wisdom.[13]

The correlation between the epic of Gilgamesh and coaching lies in the transformative nature of Gilgamesh's journey. As the story unfolds, Gilgamesh experiences a core shift, gaining astuteness, humility, and a correct perception of the human condition.

Coaching does something very similar, which calls for an inner human revolution by rising above the ego-centric tendencies that halt one's growth.

The story of Gilgamesh offers valuable lessons that can be applied to coaching:

A) **Courageously Authentic:** Gilgamesh's journey exposes his vulnerability and makes him confront the limitations of his power. Likewise, coaching urges clients to welcome their authenticity, thus finding the courage to face their fears, uncertainties and limitations. By acknowledging and accepting their authentic selves, clients can draw on their inner power.

B) **Self-reflection:** Throughout the epic, Gilgamesh engages in self-inquiry. Coaching assists clients in developing self-awareness, allowing them to reflect on their values, beliefs, and behaviours. This self-reflection helps clients make clearer conscious choices and tune their actions with their true selves.

Here is a quote from the *Epic of Gilgamesh* that reflects Gilgamesh's introspection and contemplation:

"I am going to die, and I do not know what death will be like. I wander around in the wilderness because I am terrified of death. Who has gone up to heaven and come down? Who has obtained the knowledge of all things? I will enter the house of dust—I will go to the dwelling of darkness, to the palace where the dead dwell and where those who once ruled the world lie sleeping—where they do not hear the voice of the living. I am afraid of death, so I roam the wilderness and pray to the gods to help me confront my fear." (*Epic of Gilgamesh*, Tablet IX.)[14]

In this passage, Gilgamesh reflects upon his mortality and expresses his fear of death. It showcases his quest for understanding the mysteries of life and the afterlife. For us is to focus on his introspective nature.

And how would it be if Gilgamesh met a coach like yourself today?

The following fictional coaching session portrays a possible short interaction between Gilgamesh as the client and a modern coach, who digs deep into his thoughts and seeks a way forward:

Coach: "Welcome, Gilgamesh. I'm here to partner with you to help you confront your fear of the unknown. Let's begin by discussing your thoughts and emotions surrounding the concept of mortality. How would you describe your current understanding of the impermanence of life?"

Gilgamesh: "I am aware that one day, I will pass away but I feel a deep uncertainty about what comes after death. This uncertainty has led me to question the purpose of my existence. Can you guide me in finding clarity amidst these contemplations?"

Coach: "Absolutely, Gilgamesh. The fear of the unknown and the search for meaning are common aspects of the human experience. Let's take a close look at your fear of death. What specific aspects of the afterlife or the end of life are most unsettling for you? Is it the idea of leaving everything behind or the uncertainty of what lies beyond?"

Gilgamesh: "I fear the mystery that shrouds death. I wonder if anyone has ever found what awaits us after we leave this world. It feels like entering a realm of silence and darkness, detached from the voices of the living. How can I find peace amidst this uncertainty?"

Coach: "Your curiosity about the mysteries of life and the afterlife is a natural part of the human thirst for meaning and understanding. Let's scan your beliefs and perceptions surrounding life's impermanence. What are your current ideas and views about the nature of life after death? Are there any cultural, philosophical or spiritual perspectives that resonate with you?"

Gilgamesh: *"I have heard tales of heroes and rulers who have passed away, and enter a realm where the departed reside. I seek to know the unknown. How can I reconcile my mortality with the desire to live a purposeful and rewarding life?"*

Coach: *"Your contemplations show a deep yearning for understanding and purpose. Let's pore over some ways to confront your fear of the unknown and find meaning in the face of mortality. How can you accept the inevitability of death as a catalyst for living a more intentional life? Are there any actions or outlooks you would see as options?"*

Gilgamesh: *"I want to find the courage within myself to face this fear and live a life of significance. I want to make the most of my time here and leave a telling legacy. How can I do it?"*

Coach: *"Your desire for courage and purpose is admirable, Gilgamesh. What steps can you take to welcome uncertainty, pursue your passions and create a legacy aligned with your values?"*

Gilgamesh: *"I am ready to approach my fear with curiosity and openness."*

Coach: *"Remember, I'll be here to support you every step of the way. Together, we will negotiate and cut across your fear, uncover your inner strengths and help you find meaning in both life and the mysteries that lie beyond."*

Here's a representation of yet another fictitious dialogue that might have ensued between the characters of Gilgamesh and Enkidu from the ancient Mesopotamian epic of Gilgamesh. It is a mere interpretation to illustrate the themes of self-reflection and introspection for better understanding:

Gilgamesh: *"Enkidu, my dear friend, why must we face such trials and tribulations? What is the purpose of our existence?"*

Enkidu: *"Gilgamesh, life is a fleeting journey filled with both joy and sorrow. We must seek wisdom and understanding to steer through it."*

Gilgamesh: *"But what is the meaning of it all? Is there more to life than power and conquest?"*

Enkidu: *"Indeed, my friend. Life is about relationships, love and the pursuit of wisdom. It is through these experiences that we find purpose and fulfilment."*

Gilgamesh: *"I have been consumed by my pride and ambition. I yearn for something greater—something that transcends my mortal existence."*

Enkidu: *"You have the capacity for greatness, Gilgamesh. It lies not in the pursuit of immortality or power but in the connections you forge and the legacy you leave behind."*

Gilgamesh: *"I must start a journey of self-discovery to confront my fears and limitations. Only then can I find true meaning and transform into a better version of myself."*

Enkidu: *"Go, my friend, and may your journey bring you the wisdom and understanding you seek. Remember, it is in self-reflection and introspection that we uncover our true selves."*

This imagined dialogue between Gilgamesh and Enkidu serves to illustrate the inner turmoil and yearning for the purpose that Gilgamesh experiences. It highpoints his willingness to engage in soul-searching to find answers. The dialogue also accentuates the importance of relationships, one's evolution and the seeking of wisdom, which are essential aspects of coaching and individual progress.

C) **Ephemeral and the Absolute:** The epic of Gilgamesh brings to us the theme of mortality and the transient nature of life. Coaching gently nudges clients to consider this reality of impermanence to let go of trivial concerns and find meaning and purpose in the here and now, by letting go of fear and resistance. They learn to be agile to the ever-changing nature of life and find new possibilities amidst uncertainty.

They shift their focus from external goals and societal expectations to what truly matters to them on a personal and authentic level and generate absolute happiness that is independent of external circumstances.

In the fast-paced and ever-changing modern world, that often values a culture of urgency, constant progress and achievement, the theme of impermanence thus holds great relevance. It underscores the significance of letting go of the pressure to constantly strive for more and instead have gratitude for the present moment and what it brings.

In conclusion, this tale serves as a timeless reminder that our time on Earth is limited, and it is up to each individual to make the most of it.

D) **Cords of Committed Connection**: In the modern corporate context, the importance of building heartfelt connections with others, just as Gilgamesh did in his friendship with Enkidu, cannot be overstated. Coaching underscores the value of building real relationships and the great impact they can have on success.

In today's corporate world, collaboration, teamwork, and effective relationships are essential for achieving organizational goals and a positive work culture. Investing in cordial relationships with colleagues, superiors and subordinates can enhance communication, trust and cooperation, which can lead to increased productivity and innovation. The ingredients for the latter are mutual respect, positive regard and making the other person feel valued. The key to making these relationships grow involves building on elements of honesty to help create that lasting foundation.

Coaching plays a vital role here. Clients explore their interpersonal skills, emotional intelligence and communication styles, to build rapport and resolve conflicts within their professional environments.

By drawing parallels to Gilgamesh's friendship with Enkidu, coaches can highlight the value of authentic connections in the corporate world. Enkidu's friendship had an undeniable impact on Gilgamesh's journey, which transformed him from a self-centred king into a compassionate and empathetic leader. Similarly, authentic relationships in the workplace can bring out the best in individuals.

Coaches can assist clients in developing networking skills and cultivating relationships that go beyond superficial interactions. They can further help clients identify common interests, shared values and areas of collaboration with colleagues and stakeholders.

Additionally, coaches can also support clients in developing leadership skills that centre around relationship-building and efficacious communication.

To conclude, the impact of these connections extends beyond individual growth, positively influencing team dynamics, organizational culture, and ultimately, the success and well-being of the entire corporate ecosystem.

The epic in totality serves as a reminder that change is possible, even in the face of difficulties and the inherent imperfections of being human. And that coaching is not only about achieving external success but also about building inner strength, and the realization of one's true purpose and potential.

Beyond the realms of Greek mythology and the epic of Gilgamesh, there exists a treasure trove of ancient myths from diverse cultures, such as Babylonian, Sumerian, and Incan that provide intriguing semblances to the origins and principles of coaching.

From the mystic lands of Babylon, we stumble upon the tales of gods and heroes, which unpack the dynamics between power and humility, as well as leadership and guidance. The Sumerian myths transport us to a time when humans and deities walked side by side, giving us a peek into the human longing to make meaning of everything. And with the Incan civilization, we come across sagas of wisdom keepers and celestial beings, aligning with the modern principles of coaching.

Now, let us look into these ancient myths and uncover their significance in relation to coaching:

Babylonian and Sumerian Myths: Inanna is a Mesopotamian goddess who is worshipped in ancient Sumerian and Akkadian cultures. Her story and mythological significance have roots in the Mesopotamian region. The myth of the goddess Inanna's descent into the underworld is awe-inspiring and analogous to our inner revolution. As Inanna descends into the underworld, she is stripped of her outer identities, symbols of power and worldly attachments. This symbolic act of shedding represents letting go of the roles and expectations society places on us, as well as releasing attachments to material possessions and superficial pursuits. In today's world, we often wear masks to conform to societal norms or to present a certain image to others. This act of shedding isn't about becoming less, but about releasing what no longer serves us so that we can discover and embrace the core of who we are.

It further mirrors the casting off of tendencies that limit us from being who we can be or wish to be and awakening to our inner strength by overcoming the fundamental darkness that resides within us in the form of ego, self-doubt, self-deprecation, other fancies and illusions. Throughout her journey, Inanna faces many trying tests, as well as experiences death, rebirth, and resurrection. These trials and transformations denote the churning that individuals undertake in the coaching process. However, from the way Inanna emerges from this stirring event, we too can rise to face our fears, trials and tribulations, and gain a clearer understanding of ourselves and our place in the world.

The story concludes with Inanna's return from the underworld to the world of the living. However, during her return, she must choose someone to take her place in the underworld as a substitute. In some versions of the myth, she chooses her lover, Dumuzid.

This cyclical nature of the episode signifies Inanna's integration of the underworld experiences into her being.[15] This mythic ending carries the message that exploring the depths of one's being often involves confronting the shadows within ourselves which are also sometimes the central aspects of the coaching journey.

In modern life, the cyclical journey of Inanna's story can be likened to the process of individuals facing challenges, undergoing transformation, and then returning to their daily lives stronger and wiser. This cycle shows that personal development isn't linear; it involves revisiting and integrating lessons, much like how our growth doesn't happen in a straight line.

Incan Mythology: In the Incan myth of Viracocha, we encounter a vivid reflection of the coaching role. Viracocha, the creator deity, is not only responsible for shaping the physical world but also for sharing knowledge and instilling moral and ethical values that elevate humanity. This resonates with the coach's role in supporting individuals toward growth and transformation. Viracocha is often depicted as a bearded figure wearing a long robe and carrying a staff or a sceptre.

According to Incan beliefs, Viracocha emerged from the waters of Lake Titicaca and brought forth the sun, moon, stars, and human beings. This act symbolizes not only the birth of celestial bodies but also that of light and illumination. In the context of coaching, the parallel is striking—just as Viracocha brings forth the sun's light, coaches help individuals shine their inner light, their untapped potential.

He is also believed to have imparted the knowledge of various arts, sciences and agricultural practices, which have contributed to the development of civilization. This finds its counterpart in coaches contributing to the advancement of the individual and, in a broader sense, the community.[16]

In the context of coaching, the myth of Viracocha can be seen as a metaphorical representation of the coach as a catalyst for change. Like Viracocha, coaches have the ability to facilitate the creation of new possibilities and help individuals nurture their inner brilliance.

Finally, Viracocha's role as a creator figure aligns with the coaching process of helping individuals shape their lives and create their desired reality.

Hindu [Indian] Mythology: We can never conclude this discussion without sharing one of the finest examples from Indian ancient Hindu mythology that parallels the coaching process. It is the story of Lord Krishna guiding Arjuna, in an epic dialogue, on the battlefield of Kurukshetra in the Bhagavad Gita.

Picture the scene: A vast battlefield, not just of swords and arrows, but of inner conflict. The air charged with tension, and the weight of moral conflict hanging heavy in the air. In the midst of this, stands Arjuna, a warrior prince, grappling with a crisis of conscience. He's torn between duty and compassion, honour and the horror of war. He is faced with the moral dilemma of fighting in a war that involves his own kin and loved ones. He is overwhelmed by doubt, confusion, and a sense of helplessness.

Enter Lord Krishna, not as a divine figure to be revered, but as a guide, a coach, a friend. In the Bhagavad Gita, Krishna becomes Arjuna's confidant in this moment of doubt. Their dialogue in the Bhagavad Gita isn't just a sacred text; it's a coaching session that bridges ancient wisdom with modern understanding.

Krishna listens, not just with his ears, but with empathy. He doesn't impose solutions; he invites introspection. Arjuna's doubts, his turmoil, find resonance in our own battles of doubt and confusion. Sound familiar?

It's a struggle that resonates with anyone facing life's complex choices.

He asks Arjuna to explore his values, ambitions, and fears. One of the most powerful moments is when Krishna says, "You have the right to work, but never to the fruit of work." Here, Krishna is coaching Arjuna to focus on his actions and his efforts, rather than being overly attached to outcomes—a core tenet of coaching today. Just as a modern coach might say, "Focus on what you can control."

Krishna's words transform Arjuna's perspective. He empowers Arjuna to rise above his doubts, reclaim his purpose, and embrace his duty. He says, "Perform your obligatory duty, for action is better than inaction." It's a sentiment that reverberates in modern coaching—take steps, even in adversity.[17]

This exchange exemplifies coaching's essence—a companion who empowers and helps individuals align with their core values. The Bhagavad Gita shows that even in the midst of immense challenges, coaching, in its essence, existed centuries ago. It's about support, growth, and discovering our inner strength. Just as Krishna guided Arjuna, modern coaching helps us traverse life's battlefield, enabling us to make choices with clarity, purpose, and courage.

Ancient myths, such as those from Indian, Greek, Babylonian, Sumerian, and Incan cultures offer weighty peeks into the themes of self-realisation and transformation. Coaching provides individuals with a framework to examine their narratives, surmount difficulties and unlock their innate potential, just as the myths guided heroes on their journeys—a universal archetype, to discover inner strengths, and return with wisdom and gifts. Coaches serve as thinking partners, and support clients through their own hero's journeys, thus helping them leverage their unique strengths and integrate their inner shifts into their lives.

By using the wisdom and symbolism of these ancient myths as metaphors, coaches can expand their coaching practice, tap into the wisdom of the ages and provide clients with powerful tools.

Please note that while the concepts and parallels mentioned here are inspired by various mythologies, it is essential to approach mythology with respect and acknowledge that interpretations may vary across different cultural and scholarly perspectives.

Principles of Coaching:

Coaching is guided by a set of principles that underpin its practice. These principles create a structure for coaches to carry out their coaching practice. Some key principles include:

a) **Client-centred Approach**: Coaching places the client at the centre, honouring their uniqueness, values, and goals. The coach adopts a non-directive stance, empowering the client rather than providing advice or solutions.

In the dialogue below, the coach and coachee engage in a candid discussion about hardships, values and aspirations. The coach actively listens and collaborates with Adam to create an action plan, which will help him find a more fulfilling career. The conversation maintains a client-centric approach, which allows Adam to express his thoughts and emotions openly while the coach provides needed assistance.

Example:

Coach: "Good morning, Adam. How have you been since our last session?"

Adam: "Honestly, I've been struggling a bit. I feel overwhelmed by the demands of my job and I'm not finding the fulfilment I hoped for."

Coach: "I understand, Adam. It's common to face struggles and reassess our goals along the way. Let's take some time to reflect on what truly matters to you in your career and see how we can create a more fulfilling path for you. What are some values that are important to you?"

Adam: "Well, I've always valued growth and learning. I want to feel like I'm making a difference and contributing to something meaningful. And work-life balance is becoming increasingly important to me."

Coach: "Thank you for sharing, Adam. It's great that you're aware of these values. Let's understand how you can typify these values in your career. Can you give me an example of a time when you felt a strong sense of fulfilment and alignment with your values at work?"

Adam: "I remember, when I worked on a project that focused on sustainability, it was incredibly rewarding to be part of something that made a positive impact on the environment. I felt truly alive and motivated during that time."

Coach: "That's wonderful, Adam. It's clear that making a positive impact and working in a field aligned with sustainability are important to you. How can we *leverage your experience and skills to explore career options that incorporate these values?"*

Adam*: "I think I could explore opportunities in the renewable energy sector or even consider working for an organization with a strong corporate social responsibility focus."*

Coach*: "Those sound like promising directions, Adam. Let's work together to create an action plan that will help you transition into a more fulfilling and balanced career. What can we consider?"*

Adam*: "I want to work on my networking opportunities, update my resume and develop strategies for interviews and job applications. Does that sound good?"*

Coach*: "That sounds great, Adam. Remember, this coaching process is about you taking ownership of your career and making choices that are in tune with your values and aspirations. I'm here with you every step of the way."*

b) **Confidentiality and Trust**: A coaching relationship is built on trust, confidentiality and mutual respect. Coaches create a sacred space where clients can express their thoughts, emotions and aspirations without fear of disclosure.

Example:

Client*: "I've been struggling with an overbearing boss who constantly micromanages me. It's affecting my productivity and confidence at work."*

Coach*: "I understand how perplexing that can be. It's important for you to have a safe space to discuss this issue. I want you to know that confidentiality is a fundamental principle in coaching. As your coach, I am committed to upholding strict confidentiality guidelines and I will not disclose any information without your explicit permission."*

Client*: "That's reassuring to hear, thank you. I have some sensitive topics I want to share, and it's important to me that they remain private, without any fear of repercussions. I've been hesitant to discuss this matter because it's a workplace situation and I'm concerned. However, I now feel confident to seek a way forward without any reservations."*

Coach: *"You're most welcome. Trust is the keystone of our coaching relationship. Let's now focus on crafting effective approaches that will help you fruitfully deal with your overbearing boss and create a work environment that's both uplifting and conducive to productivity."*

It is important to recognize that confidentiality goes beyond mere words. The true intent to maintain privacy and discretion can be sensed by the client at a somatic or neuropsychological level. As a coach, it is not only about promising confidentiality but also about creating a safe and trustworthy space where the client feels a genuine sense of security. When the coach lives this principle, the client perceives it on a deeper level, which allows them to open up, and engage in the coaching process with confidence. Confidentiality, therefore, becomes an embodied commitment that builds the foundation of trust and leads to a productive coaching relationship.

Professional coaching organizations, such as the International Coach Federation (ICF), underscore the ethical principle of confidentiality and its role in maintaining client trust.[18] It is therefore a must for coaches to adhere to professional codes of ethics and maintain the confidentiality of client information. By doing so, coaches uphold the ethical standards of the coaching profession.

Numerous studies have explored the impact of trust and confidentiality in various therapeutic settings, which highlight their positive effects on client engagement, disclosure and therapeutic outcomes. While these studies may not be specific to coaching, they provide insights into the broader context of confidentiality and its significance in promoting trust and openness in client-centred relationships.

c) **Goal Orientation**: Coaching is future-focused, which helps clients clarify their goals, aspirations and vision for themselves. Clients co-create meaningful and achievable goals in line with their values and purpose.

Example:

Coach: "Good morning, Noha. How can I support you today?"

Noha: "Good morning, Coach. I'm dealing with a colleague whose behaviour is crippling our team's productivity. Every time I see her, I cringe and go into my shell."

Coach: "I understand the challenge, Noha. What do you envision for your team's dynamics and productivity?"

Noha: "I want to create a more collaborative and efficient work environment where everyone feels valued and championed."

Coach: "That's a great goal, Noha. Now, let's discuss actionable steps you can take to address this behaviour and infuse positivity."

Noha: "I think having a direct conversation with my colleague, expressing my concerns and establishing clear expectations would be a good start."

Coach: "Excellent. Let's work on setting boundaries to address the behaviour constructively. What could be some effective communication strategies you could explore? Remember, the goal is to create a productive work environment."

Noha: "I'm committed to resolving this issue and improving our team's morale."

Coach: "I believe in your ability to make a positive impact, Noha."

In this brief coaching dialogue, the coach assists Noha in addressing the stifling behaviour of a colleague at work. The attention is on clarifying Noha's desired outcome and setting actionable goals. The coach subtly nudges Noha to shift her focus from the past to the present and attain what she is striving for.

d) **Accountability and Action**: Coaching emphasizes accountability and action motivating clients to take responsibility for their growth, as well as providing feedback and inspiration to help them move forward.

One real-life example that highlights the principle of accountability and action in coaching comes from a study by Grant, Curtayne, and

Burton (2009).[19] The study examined the effectiveness of coaching in improving goal attainment and subjective well-being.

In the study, participants were divided into two groups—a coaching group and a control group. The coaching group received regular coaching sessions where they set specific goals, identified action steps, and received assistance and feedback from their coach. The control group did not receive coaching.

The results showed that the coaching group demonstrated significantly higher goal attainment and subjective well-being compared to the control group. The participants in the coaching group credited their success to the sense of accountability and the structured action plans developed during the sessions. They reported feeling more driven and determined and enabled to take action towards their goals.

This example illustrates how coaching, with its weight on accountability and action, can have a significant impact on clients' goal attainment and help achieve meaningful results.

Core Competencies of Coaching:

Coaching is a skill-based profession that requires mastery of specific competencies. These core competencies form the foundation for effective coaching. They include:

Active Listening: Coaches practice active listening, paying full attention to the client—not only to their words but also to their emotions, body language, tone, facial expressions, slight shifts in movement and posture, and underlying messages. This level of listening allows coaches to gain a comprehensive understanding of the client's needs, challenges and aspirations.

A Zen Story That Highlights the Importance of Active Listening:

Once, there was a Zen master who had a reputation for being a wise and compassionate listener. A young man who was going through a difficult time sought the master's guidance.

The young man approached the master and began pouring out his troubles—all the while talking rapidly and without pause. He talked about his problems, his fears and his confusion and hardly took a breath. The master listened attentively, nodding occasionally but said nothing. After some time, the young man stopped talking, exhausted from expressing all his thoughts and emotions. He looked at the master, waiting for his wise counsel.

The master smiled and asked, "Do you want a cup of tea?"

Confused, the young man replied, "Uh, yes, thank you."

The master poured the tea into a cup and continued to pour even after the cup was full, allowing the tea to overflow and spill onto the table.

The young man, feeling astonished, exclaimed, "Master, the cup is overflowing! It can't hold any more tea!"

The master calmly responded, "Just like this cup, your mind is overflowing with thoughts and emotions. You need to empty it before it can receive anything new. Active listening is like emptying your cup and creating space for understanding and insight."

The young man realized the wisdom in the master's words. He had been so caught up in his thoughts and concerns that he had not truly listened to himself or others. The experience taught him the importance of being fully present, attentive, and open to receiving what others have to say without judgement or interruption.

From that day forward, the young man practised active listening in his interactions with others, thus allowing them to express themselves fully. In doing so, he discovered that truly hearing others, having meaningful connections, and showing empathy are all but interconnected.

This Zen story reminds us that *active listening* involves setting aside our preconceptions and distractions, giving our undivided attention to the speaker and allowing evocative communication to flourish.

Reflection and Powerful Questioning: Coaches employ powerful questioning and reflective inquiry techniques to stimulate deep reflection and self-discovery in clients. Reflective inquiry involves skilfully guiding clients to explore their thoughts, emotions and experiences in a non-judgemental and curious manner. By asking thought-provoking questions and getting clients to connect with their inner wisdom, coaches facilitate this process. Reflective inquiry helps clients view things from a clear lens, and uncover hidden patterns, thus enabling them to make more informed decisions and take purposeful action in harmony with their aspirations and core principles.

Additionally, when coaches summarize what the client has shared, it serves as a form of reflective inquiry, which allows clients to validate their insights and gain clarity. By reflecting back on the client's words and experiences, coaches create an environment for further probing. This integrated approach of questioning and reflective inquiry greatly empowers the clients.

In a coaching session, the coach might use a question/s to trigger reflective inquiry to get the client to introspect and develop a fresh outlook in the following way:

Coach: "Adam, as we discussed your career aspirations, what are some underlying beliefs or assumptions that may be influencing your current situation?"

Adam: "Well, I've always believed that success means climbing the corporate ladder and earning a high salary. But lately, I've been questioning whether that's truly what makes me happy."

Coach: "I appreciate your honesty, Adam. Let's plunge head-on into this. What experiences or moments have caused you to question the connection between success and personal happiness?"

This process of self-reflection is a powerful tool.

a) **Goal Setting**: Coaches facilitate the process of setting clear, specific and attainable goals with clients. It involves identifying the client's desired outcomes, breaking them down into actionable steps and creating a roadmap. Coaches help clients clarify their priorities, uncover any potential barriers and develop strategies to overcome them. By establishing well-defined goals, clients gain a sense of direction.

b) **Feedback and Support**: Coaches provide feedback and support that are timely, constructive and non-judgemental. They inspire, celebrate progress, and help clients identify areas for improvement.

A Buddhist parable to illustrate it:

A young disciple approached his master seeking guidance on his spiritual journey. The master took the disciple to a lush garden filled with various plants and flowers. The master pointed to a bamboo tree and said, "Observe the bamboo tree and learn from it."

Curious, the disciple observed the bamboo tree's tall and slender form and its graceful swaying in the wind. The master explained, "The bamboo tree teaches us about feedback and support—two vital elements for personal development."

The disciple pondered this and asked, "But how does the bamboo tree receive feedback and support?"

With a serene smile, the master responded, "In the presence of a gentle breeze, the bamboo tree adapts, much like individuals adjust when encouraged. And when fierce winds arrive, the tree's deep roots and flexibility enable it to stand resilient. It uses its inner strength and connection to the earth to endure."

The disciple grasped the metaphor: the winds, like feedback and support, come in diverse forms. The gentle breeze embodies encouragement, bolstering confidence, while the robust wind of constructive feedback challenges individuals to stretch their boundaries and evolve.

In the realm of coaching, the significance becomes clear. Coaches offer observations and perspectives that assist clients in a multitude of ways.

c) **Intuition and Presence**: Coaches cultivate their intuition and presence, thus developing an attuned awareness of the client's needs and emotions. This allows them to respond authentically and adapt their coaching approach to best serve the client's growth. [Intuition is discussed in detail in the next chapter.]

The Coaching Relationship:

Relationships are at the heart of the human experience. The undeniable impact of relationships extends to all dimensions of our lives, which encompass our physical, emotional, mental, and spiritual well-being.

They shape our sense of identity, influence our beliefs and values and contribute to our overall happiness and fulfilment. In personal relationships, they provide us with a sense of belonging, love and support. In professional settings, they enable collaboration, effective communication, and teamwork.

When it comes to coaching, the quality of the coaching relationship significantly influences the effectiveness and outcomes of the coaching process. In the realm of personal growth, nurturing healthy relationships augments our self-esteem, self-worth, and self-confidence. When we feel seen, heard, and understood by others, we develop a greater sense of self-awareness and acceptance. This self-awareness is a crucial foundation for coaching, as it allows clients to enquire into their values, strengths and areas for development with an unclouded lens.

Emotionally, strong relationships offer a sense of connection, and let us express and process our emotions. In the coaching relationship, clients experience a similar level of support and a compassionate presence. This enables clients to scour through their inner world more deeply, thus leading to multi-dimensional benefits.

Mentally, positive relationships contribute to our cognitive development, critical thinking, and problem-solving abilities. Engaging in meaningful conversations and exchanging ideas with others expands our perspective, stimulates our intellect, and broadens our knowledge. In coaching, the coach-client relationship becomes a catalyst for clients to expand their mental horizons.

On a spiritual level, tending relationships brings interconnectedness and purpose. They remind us of our shared humanity and the importance of contributing to something greater than ourselves. In coaching, the coaching relationship just does the same. While it might not directly mirror the depth of spiritual interconnectedness, it can still provide a sense of purpose and connection to personal goals and growth. Ultimately, the coaching relationship serves as a powerful catalyst for a holistic change as it brings together the various dimensions of our being fashioning a life of greater joy.

Thus, we can see that in the context of coaching, the coaching relationship forms the basis of the entire process. In coaching, the relationship is the vehicle through which coaching goals are achieved. It is a dynamic and collaborative partnership between the coach and the client and is characterized by unconditional positive regard, which allows the clients to explore, reflect and grow.

As a coach, cultivating such a coaching relationship is paramount. It requires a genuine commitment to the well-being of the client.

Integrating Coaching and Buddhism:

Coaching and Buddhism share common principles and values, thus making them complementary approaches. Both emphasize an inquiry of beliefs and perspectives.

Extensive research has shown that the integration of Buddhist principles into coaching practices can have a profound impact on personal transformation. Studies have demonstrated that incorporating mindfulness and self-awareness techniques, derived from Buddhism, can enhance clients' well-being, emotional regulation, and overall life satisfaction (Davidson et al. 2003; Shapiro, Carlson, Astin and Freedman, 2006).[20]

Moreover, empirical evidence suggests that the cultivation of compassion and non-attachment in coaching fosters a therapeutic alliance, which is characterized by a great understanding of human nature (Fletcher and Jones, 2019; Siegel, Germer, and Olendzki, 2009).[21] This alliance, rooted in Buddhist values leads to transformative outcomes.

The convergence of coaching and Buddhism not only offers an evidence-based approach to personal growth but also aligns with contemporary theories and practices in positive psychology, mindfulness-based interventions and holistic well-being (Bohlmeijer, Prenger, Taal, and Cuijpers, 2010; Fredrickson et al., 2008; Lyubomirsky, King, and Diener, 2005).[22] The blend of these disciplines provides a comprehensive framework for coaches to facilitate clients' journeys.

Conclusion:

Chapter 3 has provided an overview of the canonicals of coaching. We have explored the origins, principles, and core competencies that underpin the coaching profession. The chapter has stressed the importance of the coaching relationship, active listening, powerful questioning, goal setting, and feedback in facilitating personal growth and development.

By combining these two disciplines, coaches can consolidate their grasp and expand their repertoire of techniques, thus enabling them to provide even more effective support to their clients.

You yourself must strive. The Buddhas only point the way.

– Buddha

The Intersection of Buddhism and Coaching

Chapter 4

The Empathic Edge

Here is an example of a compassionate mindset in action by a global figure:

Nelson Mandela, the renowned South African leader and anti-apartheid activist, demonstrated a remarkable display of compassion during his Presidency. After years of being imprisoned for his activism, Mandela emerged with a mindset of forgiveness and reconciliation. Instead of seeking revenge or retribution, he pursued a path of unity and healing for his country.

One notable example is Mandela's approach to the Truth and Reconciliation Commission (TRC), which was established to address the human rights violations committed during the apartheid era. Mandela recognized the importance of allowing both victims and perpetrators to share their stories and seek forgiveness. With compassion and understanding as the backdrop, he aimed at promoting healing, appeasement and building a more inclusive society.

Mandela's compassionate attitude and commitment to forgiveness played a significant role in the peaceful transition from apartheid to democratic South Africa. His leadership and emphasis on compassion continue to inspire people around the world.[23]

In Chapter 4, we shift the spotlight onto the attributes and outlook that define a compassionate coach. We analyse how these characteristics can whittle our coaching approach and get clients to thrive.

We learn more of self-compassion practices, of forgiveness and prevail over self-criticism, thus highlighting how these aspects contribute to a robust coaching dynamic when we coach the whole person.

But who is a compassionate coach?

Picture this—coaches who embody empathy and radiate genuine care for their client's well-being. They possess a remarkable ability to listen beyond words, thus tuning into the unspoken emotions that lie beneath the surface.

Through real-life examples that will leave you awe-inspired, you will witness the magic that unfolds when compassionate coaches forge real connections with their clients, unveil new possibilities for behavioural change and help them make headway.

I shall introduce you to Sara, a coach who effortlessly creates a safe space for her clients to share their deep-seated fears and dreams. But our exploration does not stop there. We peek into the compassionate coach's mindset, thus ascertaining the invaluable role of self-compassion in the coaching relationship. You will meet Mark, a coach who recognizes the importance of self-care and models it for his clients. Prepare to be inspired by Mark's journey.

Through the lens of relatable metaphors, we marvel at the awakening to the power of forgiveness through the coaching partnership. You shall encounter Lisa, a coach who helps her clients grasp the impact of forgiveness and liberates them from the burdens of the past to pave the way for healing and subsequent forward movement.

Are you ready to immerse yourself in the stories, metaphors and wisdom that will elevate your coaching practice to new heights of compassion and effectiveness?

Sara—The Empathy Catalyst

Sara, a compassionate coach known for her empathetic approach, sits across from her client Emily. Emily is struggling with self-doubt and fears that are holding her back from pursuing her dreams.

Sara: "Emily, from what you just said, I can sense that there's something weighing heavily on your mind. Would you like to share what's been bothering you?"

Emily: "Sara, I've always dreamed of starting my own business, but I'm filled with self-doubt. I fear that I'll fail, and it's been paralyzing me."

Sara: "Emily, thank you for opening up and sharing your dreams and fears with me. Your aspirations are important, and it's natural to feel uncertain when stepping into something new. I want you to know that I believe in your abilities and potential."

Emily: "That means a lot, Sara. But how can I overcome these doubts and fears?"

Sara: "Emily, let's examine your fears together. What beliefs are fuelling your self-doubt? What is that one step you can work on to shift them to empowering beliefs?"

Emily: "I appreciate your support, Sara. [silence] Yes, I have been holding onto an instance from the past…"

Sara's empathetic approach instils a sense of trust and validation, which allows Emily to open up and explore her self-doubt. With Sara's guidance, Emily begins to question her limiting beliefs and finds the courage to pursue her dreams.

Mark—The Self-compassion Trailblazer

Mark, a compassionate coach with a strong focus on self-compassion, engages in a dialogue with his client Jason, who is struggling with overwhelming stress and self-criticism.

Mark: "Jason, as I hear you, it seems like you're carrying a heavy burden. Tell me, how have you been taking care of yourself amidst all the stress?"

Jason: "Honestly, Mark, I've been neglecting myself. I keep pushing myself to meet unrealistic expectations, and I'm constantly berating myself for any perceived failures."

Mark: "Jason, it's crucial to recognize that you deserve compassion and care, just like anyone else. Let's consider ways to integrate self-compassion practices into your daily life. By cultivating self-kindness and embracing imperfection, you can develop a healthier relationship with yourself and alleviate the weight of self-criticism."

Mark helps Jason understand the importance of self-compassion as a means of sustaining his well-being. Through guided exercises and reflective dialogues, Mark supports Jason in shifting his self-talk and cultivating a mindset of self-acceptance and self-care.

Exercise 1: Self-compassion Talk

Exercise 2: Self-compassion Break

Exercise to process painful events and negative emotions more healthfully:

Think of a situation in your life that is difficult, which is causing you stress. Call the situation to mind and see if you can actually feel the stress and emotional discomfort in your body. The intent is not to relive the hurt or pain but to become aware of and accept the difficult emotions in your body.

Now, say to yourself:

1. This is a moment of suffering.

   That's mindfulness. Other options include:

   - This hurts.

   - Ouch.

   - This is stress.

   Now, breathe out and let go.

2. Suffering is a part of life.

   That's common to humanity. Other options include:

   - Other people feel this way too.

   - I'm not alone.

   - We all struggle in our lives.

   Now, put your hands over your heart, feel the warmth of your hands and the gentle touch of your hands on your chest. Or adopt the soothing touch you discovered felt right for you.

3. May I be kind to myself.

   This is self-compassion.

   You can also ask yourself, "What do I need to hear right now to express kindness to myself?" Is there a phrase that speaks to you in your particular situation, such as:

   - May I give myself the compassion that I need.

   - May I learn to accept myself as I am.

   - May I forgive myself.

   - May I be strong.

   - May I be patient.

This practice can be used any time of day or night and will help you remember to evoke the three aspects of self-compassion when you need it most.

The Healing Power of Forgiveness: Lisa— "The Forgiveness Architect"

Lisa, a compassionate coach with a focus on forgiveness, engages in a conversation with her client Michael, who is struggling with bitterness and resentment towards a past relationship.

Lisa: "Michael, it seems like there's unresolved pain from your past that's still affecting you. Can you share a little bit about what you're holding onto?"

Michael: "Lisa, I went through a difficult divorce, and the resentment I feel towards my ex-spouse is eating away at me. I can't seem to move forward."

Lisa: "Michael, I invite you to reflect on your current emotional state. How does holding onto resentment towards your ex-spouse impact your overall well-being and happiness?"

Michael: "It's been weighing me down and affecting my ability to move forward."

Lisa: "Thank you for sharing that. It sounds like finding a path towards forgiveness could be beneficial for your personal growth. Can you recall any instances where you've experienced forgiveness in the past? What was the impact of forgiveness on your well-being in those situations?"

Michael: "I remember forgiving a close friend who unintentionally hurt me. It brought a sense of relief and restored our relationship."

Lisa: "That's a powerful example. Now, let's consider the potential benefits of forgiveness in your current situation. What positive changes do you envision in your life if you were able to let go of resentment and find forgiveness?"

Michael: "I think it would free up mental and emotional space and allow me to focus on my growth and happiness."

Lisa: "Absolutely. Forgiveness can create space for personal growth and emotional well-being. As we continue our coaching journey, we can consider various forgiveness practices and approaches that resonate with you. It's important to honour your unique process and readiness for forgiveness. How does that sound to you?"

Michael: "It sounds like a valuable exploration. I'm open to understanding forgiveness and its potential impact on my life."

In this dialogue, Lisa engages in open-ended questions and by avoiding prescription and honouring Michael's readiness, Lisa supports him in finding his path towards forgiveness.

There are several practical forgiveness exercises that can be used in coaching to support clients. Here are a few examples:

1. **Letter Writing**: Ask the client to write a letter to the person they want to forgive, which expresses their feelings, thoughts, and desires for healing. This exercise allows the client to release pent-up emotions and gain clarity on their forgiveness process, as well as release any lingering resentment or anger. The letter can be kept private or shared with the coach if the client feels comfortable.

2. **Perspective Shift:** Support the client to imagine stepping into the shoes of the person they want to forgive. This exercise helps the client gain empathy, thus allowing them to see the situation from a different perspective.

3. **Visualization:** Guide the client through a visualization exercise where they imagine meeting the person they want to forgive. Urge them to visualize a conversation where they seek understanding, and ultimately let go of negative emotions.

4. **Self-Forgiveness**: Explore self-forgiveness with the client by asking them to reflect on any self-blame or guilt that they may be carrying. Guide them through a process of self-compassion and acceptance, and help them release self-judgement and contemplate self-forgiveness.

5. **Gratitude Practice**: Partner with the client to focus on moments of gratitude and appreciation to help them shift their attention away from resentment and towards positive aspects of their life. This exercise can bolster a mindset of gratitude so that forgiveness can blossom.

It is important to note that the choice of forgiveness exercises should be tailored to each client's unique needs, preferences, intent, and readiness and that the effectiveness of these exercises can vary from person to person. These exercises should always be approached with sensitivity and respect for the client's emotional well-being. Supplement these exercises with ongoing support, reflection and discussion to deepen the client's understanding and integration of forgiveness in their life. Additionally, it is recommended to refer to published works and resources on forgiveness exercises for more detailed guidance and variations.

Coaches can also use metaphors as they can be powerful tools for conveying the essence of compassion. Here are a few examples:

1. **The Ripple Effect**: Compassion is often compared to a pebble dropped into a still pond, creating ripples that extend outward. Just as the ripples spread and affect the entire pond, acts of compassion have the potential to touch and positively impact the lives of many.

2. **The Warm Embrace**: Compassion is like a warm and comforting embrace that envelops and supports those in need. It provides solace, understanding and a sense of belonging.

3. **The Healing Balm**: Compassion can be likened to a soothing balm that heals wounds, both visible and invisible. Just as a healing ointment brings relief and promotes healing, compassion has the power to alleviate suffering and bring comfort.

4. **The Guiding Light**: Compassion acts as a guiding light, which illuminates the path of others who may be lost, in pain or life's vicissitudes. Like a lighthouse in the darkness, compassion provides direction and hope.

These metaphors can help convey the essence and impact of compassion in a relatable and vivid way. Let these examples inspire you to cultivate these qualities within yourself on your way to being a compassionate coach.

You may also choose to masterfully be any one of these:

1. **The Compassionate Gardener**: Just as a skilled gardener tends to each plant with care, removing weeds and providing nourishment, you can approach the clients with compassion, tailoring support to foster growth.

2. **The Compassionate Mirror:** Imagine a mirror that reflects the true essence and potential of a person without judgment or distortion. In coaching, you can be like that compassionate mirror—reflecting your clients' capabilities, principles, ambitions, and holding a space of acceptance and understanding.

3. **The Compassionate Compass**: Just as a compass aids voyagers in finding their way in unfamiliar territory, you can serve as a compassionate compass, to assist clients in finding their true north—positioning their actions and decisions with their beliefs, objectives, and genuine identity.

These roles create a deeper connection and appreciation for the compassionate approach taken by the coach.

Also, there are several published accounts of compassion demonstrated by Zen masters. Here are a few examples:

1. *The Zen Teaching of Huang Po*: The classic Zen text *On the Transmission of Mind* by Huang Po contains teachings and dialogues that accentuate the compassionate nature of Zen practice. It studies the role of compassion in guiding individuals towards liberation and awakening.[24]

2. *The Compassionate Mind:*: While not specifically focused on Zen masters, the book *A New Approach to Life's Challenges* by Paul Gilbert

delves into the concept of compassion from a psychological perspective. It discusses how cultivating compassion can enhance well-being, improve relationships, and assuage suffering.[25]

3. ***The Art of Just Sitting:*** *Essential Writings on the Zen Practice of Shikantaza* edited by John Daido Loori, a collection of writings by Zen masters explores various aspects of Zen practice, including compassion. It offers insights into how compassion is enriched through the practice of *just sitting* and its transformative effects on the practitioner.[26]

These published works provide valuable insights into the teachings and practices of Zen masters, including their perspectives on compassion. They offer readers an opportunity to deepen their understanding of compassion and its significance in Zen Buddhism.

Conclusion:

By now, we have a clear understanding of what it means to personify the compassionate coach's mindset. We have witnessed the power of empathy, self-compassion, and forgiveness in action. We have gotten equipped with practical tools and techniques to help apply them in your coaching practice.

> *Looking after oneself, one looks after others. Looking after others, one looks after oneself.*

> – Buddha

Chapter 5

The Silent Symphony

A Zen Story on Deep Listening:

Once, a young monk sought guidance from a renowned Zen master. The monk asked, "Master, what is the secret to enlightenment?"

The master replied, "Deep listening is the key."

Perplexed, the young monk inquired, "But Master, really? How does one practice deep listening?"

The master smiled and said, "Let me show you."

The master led the monk to a beautiful garden filled with chirping birds, flowing water, and rustling leaves. They sat down next to a pond, and the master closed his eyes, fully immersing himself in the sounds of nature. After a while, the master opened his eyes and asked the monk, "What do you hear?"

The monk, eager to impress him, hastily replied, "I hear the birds singing, the water flowing, and the leaves rustling."

The master shook his head and said, "No, you are only hearing the surface. Listen again."

The monk closed his eyes and took a deep breath. He let go of his thoughts and immersed himself in the sounds around him. As he listened more deeply, he began to hear the intricate melodies of the birds, the subtle nuances of the water and the gentle whispers of the leaves. Overwhelmed with awe, the monk exclaimed, "Master, I hear the symphony of nature!"

The master nodded and said, "That is deep listening. It is not merely hearing with your ears but fully engaging in it with all your senses—being present in the moment, and allowing the world to speak to you. Deep listening fosters, understanding, connection, and wisdom."

In this story, the master teaches the young monk the essence of deep listening.

In Chapter 5, we investigate the transformative power of presence and deep listening in the coaching process and build upon what we discussed in Chapter 3. We assess how the Buddha's teachings on the **relation between mindfulness and attentive listening can boost our coaching presence and deepen our connection with clients.** We will probe into mindfulness further in Chapter 8. We explore different levels of listening and the role of intuition in understanding the unspoken messages. We learn practical techniques and exercises to cultivate presence and deepen our listening skills.

Let us start with an anecdote that demonstrates the power of mindfulness.

It is the tale of Thich Nhat Hanh, a renowned Zen master and peace activist. During the Vietnam War, Thich Nhat Hanh and his fellow monks established a mindfulness retreat centre called Plum Village in southern France. This centre became a sanctuary for people seeking peace and healing, including veterans and refugees affected by the war.

In 1999, Thich Nhat Hanh was invited to speak at the United Nations Headquarters in New York City. As he addressed the audience, he shared his personal experiences of mindfulness and its transformative impact on individuals and communities. He highlighted the importance of establishing mindfulness as a practice in everyday life, promoting compassion and understanding amidst conflict.

Thich Nhat Hanh's teachings on mindfulness have resonated with people from all walks of life and inspired individuals to practice mindfulness in their own lives as well as bring about positive change. This showcases how mindfulness can transcend cultural and societal boundaries, promoting peace and resilience in the face of adversity.

To add to the testimony, here is an often-cited parable that occurs in the *Discourse on the Parable of the Water Snake (Alagaddūpama Sutta)* in the *Majjhima Nikāya* of the Pāli Canon. The parable relates to a traveller who fords a stream by paddling across it using a coracle or raft, and the Buddha asks whether it would be appropriate or not for the man to carry the raft with him once he had crossed.

This parable demonstrates the power of mindfulness:

The Story of the Raft

During one of his teachings, Buddha shared the parable of a traveller who reached the edge of a vast and treacherous river. The traveller desired to reach the other shore where enlightenment and liberation awaited him. He realized that the river was impassable without assistance. So, he gathered branches, leaves and vines to construct a makeshift raft.

As the traveller readied to go across the river, he held onto the raft tightly. The raft served as a means to safely cross the turbulent waters, but Buddha pointed out that once the traveller reached the other shore, he no longer needed to carry the raft on his back.

In this parable, *the raft represents mindfulness,* which *serves as a tool to cut through the difficulties of life.* Just as the traveller constructs a raft to safely cross the treacherous river, we develop mindfulness to wade through the choppy waters of our experiences. Mindfulness allows us to stay present, observe our thoughts and emotions, as well as respond skilfully to the circumstances we encounter.

Similar to how the traveller lets go of the raft once it has served its purpose, the essence of mindfulness is not to cling to it as an end in itself. Rather, it is about developing inner clarity and wisdom through the practice of mindfulness. Once we have developed a deeper understanding of ourselves and the nature of reality, we can release our attachment to mindfulness as a mere technique or tool. Instead, we embody mindfulness as a natural way of being, and not as a separate entity, effortlessly integrating it into our daily lives, leading to a state of liberation, peace and understanding.

Here is a model that demonstrates how mindfulness can lead to the presence and better listening in coaching:

1. **Cultivating Mindful Awareness:**

   The first step is to cultivate mindful awareness within the coaching process. It involves integrating mindfulness practices into the coach's personal routine and incorporating them into the coaching sessions.

   As a compassionate coach, the coach intentionally practices being fully present in the moment, bringing non-judgemental attention to his thoughts, emotions, and bodily sensations, setting aside distractions and immersing oneself in the client's experience. It requires suspending personal judgements, assumptions and the need to provide immediate solutions. Instead, the focus is on allowing their thoughts and emotions to unfold naturally, empowering the clients to discover their insights, solutions and strengths. It is a profound act of compassion and respect, acknowledging the client's autonomy and capacity for growth, the belief that the client is whole and resourceful. [Techniques are shared further below.]

2. **Developing Self-Reflection:**

   Through mindfulness, the coach engages in regular self-reflection and self-inquiry. Self-reflection is the practice of looking inward to examine one's thoughts, feelings, beliefs, and experiences. It involves taking time to assess one's actions, behaviours, and responses in various situations, seeking to understand what lies behind our motivations, values, and personal growth. Self-reflection promotes self-awareness, helps identify patterns, strengths, and areas for improvement, and ultimately supports personal development and better decision-making. This helps to develop their capacity for present-moment awareness and to recognize and manage any distractions that might arise during the coaching sessions.

Before the Coaching Session:

Set Intentions: Before each coaching session, coaches can set an intention to be fully present, and attentive with their clients.

They can take a moment to ground themselves, create a sense of calm and focus, as well as bring awareness to their thoughts, emotions and physical sensations. They ask themselves questions such as:

- How am I feeling right now? What emotions or sensations are present in my body?

- Am I carrying any personal biases or assumptions that could influence my perception or interactions with the client?

- What expectations or intentions do I have for this session, and am I open to adapting them based on the client's needs?

By engaging in this self-reflection, the coach creates a space of self-awareness and presence, ensuring that they enter the coaching session with a clear and open mindset.

After the Coaching Session:

After the coaching session, the coach engages in another round of self-reflection. They take a few moments to reflect on the session.

Some reflective questions they may ask themselves include:

- How did I show up for the client during the session? Was I fully present and attentive?

- Did I notice any triggers or biases that emerged during the session? How did I manage them, and how did they influence my coaching approach?

- What strengths did I bring to the session, and how can I further develop my coaching skills?

- Are there any areas where I can improve as a coach? How can I continue to develop my self-awareness and coaching effectiveness?

Through this practice, the coach strives for excellence. They become astutely aware of their coaching style, strengths, and areas for development. This ongoing self-inquiry allows the coach to refine their skills, deepen their presence, and better serve their clients in future sessions.

3. **Attuning to the Client:**

With mindful awareness and self-reflection, the coach can attune to the client's experience. They listen, not only to the client's words but also to their non-verbal cues, emotions, and underlying needs. By doing this, the coach can better understand the client's unique perspective, respond with sensitivity, and create a safe space for open communication.

4. **Suspending Judgement:**

Mindfulness helps the coach suspend judgement and approach the coaching relationship with curiosity and acceptance. Instead of jumping to conclusions, the coach practices holding a stance, which allows the client's experience to unfold without interference.

5. **Empowering Authentic Communication:**

By being mindful and present, the coach can ask insightful questions that invite the client to see their inner landscape more deeply such that the client can express themselves fully, which leads to more potent conversations and breakthroughs.

By following this model, coaches can be fully attuned to their own experience and the experience of their clients, fashioning a coaching space that serves both.

Here is a Zen story that vividly illustrates the spirit of mindfulness:

In a small Zen monastery, there was a dedicated monk named Takumi. Takumi was known for his unwavering commitment to the practice of mindfulness. One day, a new student joined the monastery and approached Takumi, eager to learn the discipline.

Takumi smiled warmly and invited the student to join him in the monastery's garden. As they walked among the vibrant flowers and swaying trees, Takumi asked the student to pick up a small pebble from the ground.

"Observe this pebble closely," Takumi instructed. "Notice its shape, weight, and texture. Feel its presence in your hand."

The student inspected the pebble, marvelling at its intricate details. Takumi then asked, "Tell me, what is the purpose of this pebble?"

Puzzled, the student replied, "Well, it doesn't seem to have a specific purpose. It's just a pebble."

Takumi nodded and said, "Exactly. This pebble exists simply as it is, without any agenda or expectations. It is fully present at this moment, and so can you be."

The student's eyes widened with realization.

Takumi continued, "Mindfulness is like this pebble in your hand. Just as the pebble is not burdened by thoughts of the past or worries about the future, mindfulness allows us to be fully present with whatever arises."

The student took the analogy of the pebble to heart and began practising mindfulness in his daily activities. Whether he was eating, walking or engaging in meditation, he embraced the present moment with an open and non-reactive mind and experienced a great sense of peace and clarity.

The story holds an important lesson to imbibe.

One proven modern model for deep listening is the *Four Levels of Listening* model developed by Otto Scharmer, a senior lecturer at MIT and author of the book, *Theory U: Leading from the Future as It Emerges.*[27]

This model is widely referenced and discussed in the field of leadership, communication and coaching:

1. **Downloading**: At this level, we listen from our preconceived notions, speculations, and judgements. We are not fully present and tend to filter information based on our existing beliefs.

2. **Factual Listening**: Factual listening involves listening to gather information and facts. We are focused on what is being said without much consideration for the emotional or relational aspects of the conversation.

3. **Empathic Listening**: Empathic listening goes beyond just gathering information. It involves empathizing with the speaker, understanding their emotions and seeing the situation from their perspective. We listen with an open heart and seek to connect on an emotional level.

4. **Generative Listening**: Generative listening is characterized by curiosity and a willingness to explore new possibilities. We listen with an open mind and let go of our agenda allowing new ideas to emerge.

Presencing is a level of listening where we connect with a larger field of awareness. We listen not only to the speaker but also to our intuition and the collective wisdom that arises. We tap into a deeper sense of knowing and allow for powerful shifts to occur.

By following this model, we can move away from surface-level listening to deep listening, which allows for a richer understanding of others and leads to change at a fundamental level.

Here are some more impactful techniques and exercises to cultivate presence and deepen listening skills as a coach:

a) **Mindful Breathing**: Before each coaching session, take a moment to focus on your breath. Inhale deeply and exhale slowly and ground yourself in the present moment. This practice helps you centre your attention and be present.

b) **Body Scan**: Close your eyes and scan your body from head to toe to notice any sensation or tension. This exercise helps you become more aware of your physical state and promotes a sense of presence.

c) **Reflective Summaries and Empathic Consideration**: After the client speaks, provide reflective summaries that capture both the content and emotions behind their words. Show empathy by acknowledging and reflecting on their feelings and experiences. This technique helps the listener clarify their understanding and provides an opportunity for the speaker to confirm or clarify their message.

d) **Silence and Pauses**: Be comfortable with moments of silence and practice intentional pauses during the conversation. Allow the client to muse and share fully. These pauses make room for deeper discernment and promote a more meaningful dialogue.

e) **Mindful Notetaking**: If you take notes during the session, do so mindfully. Take brief and relevant notes to capture key insights without getting too absorbed in writing. This allows you to maintain focus on the client's words and maintain a fuller connection.

f) **Reflective Journaling**: Engage in personal reflective journaling after coaching sessions. Explore your thoughts, reactions and observations about the coaching process. This practice enhances self-awareness and helps identify areas for improvement in your coaching skills.

g) **Mindful Listening Exercises**: Practice mindful listening outside of coaching sessions. For example, employ yourself in activities that involve actively listening to sounds in your environment or participate in guided mindfulness meditation exercises that focus on honing your ability to listen attentively.

By consistently practising these impactful techniques and exercises, you can establish a stronger connection with and understanding of the client.

While research in the field of deep listening is ongoing, here are a few emerging techniques and practices that are being explored, to help you further:

A) **Mindful Listening:** Various authors have written extensively on mindfulness, including Jon Kabat-Zinn, Thich Nhat Hanh, and Sharon Salzberg. By training our attention, we become more attuned to the speaker and the nuances of their communication.

B) **Nonviolent Communication (NVC):** Nonviolent Communication, developed by Marshall Rosenberg, emphasizes empathic listening and compassionate communication in the book, *Nonviolent Communication: A Language of Life.* It encourages active listening without judgement, which focuses on understanding the underlying needs and feelings of the speaker.[28]

C) **Appreciative Inquiry:** Appreciative Inquiry was developed by David Cooperrider and Suresh Srivastva. It is an approach that focuses on the positive aspects of a situation or individual. In deep listening, this technique involves actively seeking out the strengths, values, and ambitions expressed by the speaker and building upon them in the conversation.[29]

D) **Embodied Listening:** There are several authors and experts who discuss embodied listening, such as Peter Senge, Wendy Palmer, and Richard Strozzi-Heckler. It involves paying attention to not only the words spoken but also the speaker's body language, tone of voice, and overall presence. It requires noticing subtle cues and signals that provide additional layers of information beyond verbal communication.

E) **Narrative Listening:** Michael White and David Epston are pioneers in narrative therapy, which involves listening to and working with individual narratives. They have written books on the subject, including, *Narrative Means to Therapeutic Ends* and *Narrative Therapy in Practice: The Archaeology of Hope.*[30] Narrative listening involves attentively listening to the stories and narratives shared by speakers.

It involves understanding the personal meaning behind the story and how it shapes their worldview and experiences.

These techniques are being explored and researched to enhance our capacity for deep listening and understanding. It is important to keep in mind that the effectiveness of these techniques may vary depending on the context and individual preferences, so it is essential to adapt and customize them to fit specific coaching or communication situations.

It is also worth noting that these techniques and practices may have been influenced by multiple authors and experts in their respective fields, and their ideas are often expanded upon by various practitioners and researchers.

The War of Gut and Intuition

Intuition

It can be defined as a knowing or understanding that goes beyond conscious reasoning. It is a form of inner guidance that arises from our subconscious mind and often emerges as a feeling, a hunch, or a sense of certainty without relying on logical analysis. It taps into our accumulated knowledge, experiences and perceptions, thus enabling us to make quick and insightful judgements or decisions. Intuition can help elucidate valuable insights, perspectives and connections that may not be immediately apparent through logical thinking alone. It is a valuable tool in coaching as it helps us access hidden information and negotiate complex situations with a sense of clarity and trust.

Gut Instinct

Gut instinct, on the other hand, is a more specific and visceral response that arises from our primal instincts and survival mechanisms. It is an immediate and instinctive reaction to a situation or stimulus, often felt in the gut or the core of our being. Gut instincts are typically rapid and can be based on past experiences, learned responses or subconscious cues.

"The gut is often mistaken for intuition, but it is important to discern between the two."

While intuition and gut instinct share similarities, intuition tends to involve a broader and more nuanced understanding that may go beyond immediate survival instincts. Intuition can draw upon a deeper sense of knowing and may provide insights and guidance that go beyond immediate circumstances.

It is important to note that these terms can be subjective, and different people may use them interchangeably or with slight variations in meaning. While gut instincts are commonly experienced and recognized, it is important to note that they are not always accurate or reliable indicators of truth or optimal decision-making. Research in neuroscience suggests that gut instincts can be influenced by cognitive biases, emotions and environmental factors, which may lead to errors in judgement.

One study conducted by researchers at the University of New South Wales studied the accuracy of gut instincts in decision-making. The findings revealed that while gut instincts can sometimes lead to successful outcomes, relying solely on them without considering additional information or engaging in critical thinking can result in suboptimal decisions.

Another study published in the *Journal of Experimental Psychology: General* examined the relationship between *gut feelings* and *intuition*. The researchers found that intuitive judgements, which were based on a deeper level of unconscious processing were more accurate and reliable compared to gut instincts.[31]

These studies highlight the complexity of gut instincts and suggest that while they can provide valuable perceptions, it is important to employ reflective thinking, gather relevant information and consider multiple perspectives before making decisions. By combining gut instincts with critical thinking and intuition, individuals can enhance their decision-making abilities and make more informed choices in various aspects of life.

Intuition and its Science

The science behind intuition is a fascinating area of study that combines psychological and neurological research. While intuition is still not fully understood, here are some scientific insights that shed light on this phenomenon:

1. **Neurocognitive Processes**: Research suggests that intuition involves the integration of various cognitive processes, including pattern recognition, emotional processing, and rapid unconscious information processing. It is believed that the brain rapidly assesses and analyses vast amounts of information while drawing on past experiences and stored knowledge to arrive at intuitive insights.

2. **Emotional Intelligence**: Intuition is closely linked to emotional intelligence, which involves the ability to perceive, understand, and manage emotions effectively. Emotional intelligence enables individuals to tap into their own and others' emotional states, thus providing valuable clues and information that contribute to intuitive judgements.

3. **Implicit Learning**: Intuition is thought to be influenced by implicit learning, which refers to the unconscious acquisition of knowledge and skills without conscious awareness. Through repeated exposure to certain situations, our brains develop implicit knowledge that can inform intuitive responses.

4. **Nonconscious Information Processing**: Intuitive insights often arise from nonconscious information processing, where our brains process information without us being consciously aware. This can include picking up on subtle signs, body language, and micro-expressions that provide valuable information beyond what is communicated explicitly.

5. **Intuition and Expertise**: Experts in a particular domain often develop heightened intuition due to their extensive experience and knowledge.

This expertise allows them to make quick and accurate intuitive judgements based on a deep understanding of the subject matter.

While the science of intuition continues to evolve, these insights suggest that intuition is a complex interplay of cognitive processes, emotional intelligence, implicit learning, and nonconscious information processing. Embracing and honing our intuition can enhance our decision-making, problem-solving and understanding of others in various contexts, including coaching.

Let us look at three different coach-client scenarios as examples to understand the fair interplay between presence, inquiry and intuition:

Scenario 1:

Imagine that you are a coach working with a client who appears calm and composed on the surface but seems to be holding back something important. As you maintain a state of presence, you notice subtle shifts, a slight hesitation in their speech and a fleeting expression of sadness that quickly disappears.

You use your heightened awareness to pick up on these unspoken messages. With a compassionate and non-judgemental approach, you gently inquire, "I noticed a momentary change in your expression just now. Is there something else on your mind that you'd like to share?"

By being present, you notice the elusive cues and respond with sensitivity and curiosity. While intuition can play a role in sensing the unspoken, in this particular example, it is the coach's presence and attentive observation that facilitate the understanding of the client's unexpressed emotions and thoughts.

Scenario 2:

Imagine that you are a coach working with a client who has been struggling with making a career decision. Throughout the coaching session, he provides logical reasons for each option but seems unsure and conflicted. Despite his well-reasoned arguments, your intuition tells you that there is something deeper at play.

As you listen and engage with the client, you ask a different kind of question. Instead of focusing on the pros and cons of each option, you ask, "If you set aside all the practical considerations and external expectations, what is that you hear/see/feel?"

At that moment, you bypass the surface-level rationalization and tap into the client's inner knowing. Their response surprises them as they express a deep longing for creative expression and fulfilment, which they had been suppressing out of fear and societal pressure.

The coach's question demonstrates an inquiry-based approach to help the client access their deeper intuition. While intuition can certainly inform the coach's decision to ask that specific question, the emphasis in this example is on using inquiry as a tool to facilitate the client's self-discovery and tap into their intuitive wisdom. The coach's role is to allow the client to explore possibilities beyond the confines of logic. This breakthrough brings clarity and gets them to make a decision aligned with their true desires and values.

Scenario 3:

Coach: "I sense there's something that you haven't fully expressed. I am picking up unsureness. Would you like to share what's really going on for you?"

Client: "Well, I'm not sure how to put it into words but I have this nagging feeling that I'm not on the right path with my career. Something just doesn't feel aligned."

Coach: "I understand. Let's take a moment to pause. Close your eyes, take a deep breath and imagine yourself in a future where you're living your ideal professional life. Do you notice any sensations or images arising? What does it tell you about your true calling?"

Client: (Pauses and takes a deep breath) "You know, when I visualize that, I feel a sense of excitement and fulfilment when I imagine myself working in an artistic field, using my imaginative skills. I've always had a passion for art, but I never thought it could be a viable career option."

In this example, the coach senses that there is more to the client's situation than meets the eye and intuitively picks up on their underlying dissatisfaction. The coach then takes the client through an imaginative exercise.

The client's response reveals a deeper truth that was previously unrecognized or overlooked. It is through the coach's intuition, coupled with skilful questioning that the client is able to access his intuitive thoughts and gain clarity. Remember, intuition is a valuable resource for coaches, but it should be used in conjunction with ethical considerations, professional expertise and ongoing learning to create a supportive and transformative coaching experience.

Let us close with very real daily life examples to understand how gut and intuition may work:

Example 1

Imagine that you are walking alone at night and suddenly, you get a feeling that something is not right. Your gut instinct tells you to turn around and find another route. This immediate response is your body's natural defence mechanism to protect yourself from potential danger.

On the other hand, intuition is like a subtle inner knowing that guides you without any clear logical explanation. For example, you might have a strong intuition that a certain job opportunity is not right for you, even though everything on the surface seems favourable. It is a deep sense of knowing that comes from within, beyond what your logical mind can comprehend.

In essence, gut instinct is a swift and impulsive reaction to a particular scenario, whereas intuition is a deeper, innate understanding that steers you toward choices in harmony with your higher self.

Example 2

Imagine that you are considering a business partnership with someone. As you interact with them, you notice a nagging feeling in your gut that something is off. Despite his impressive credentials and convincing arguments, your gut instinct tells you to proceed with caution. It is a visceral response that signals a potential mismatch or red flag in the partnership.

On the other hand, intuition might come into play when you are making a decision about your career path. You may be guided by a strong inner wisdom to pursue a particular career choice that resonates with who you are, even if it defies societal expectations or seems risky on the surface.

These examples illustrate how gut instinct and intuition can play out in different aspects of life, as hunches or feelings and reflexes or perceptions, beyond what can be rationalized or explained by logic alone.

Conclusion:

Throughout this chapter, we have learnt practical techniques and exercises that serve as tools to hone the essence of presence and refine our adeptness in the art of listening. We have further learned the intricacies of various levels of listening and shed light on the invaluable role that intuition assumes in grasping unspoken messages. For a more profound exploration of the realm of mindfulness, we kindly direct readers to immerse themselves in the wisdom shared within Chapter 8.

Be where you are; otherwise, you will miss your life.

– Buddha

Chapter 6

The Sublime Conversations

Here is a story that reflects the impact of unkind and unthoughtful words.

I Take it Back

Once upon a time, a certain man went to a monk.

"Monk," he confessed, "I have been slandering you to my neighbours. I am truly sorry for what I've said and how I've treated you. I take back all the bad words that I have said. How may I find penance?"

The monk nodded graciously, then sagely proffered this command: "Go pluck three chickens. Stuff a bag with the feathers. Then, go place one feather on every doorstep in town. Return to me when you complete your task."

Scurrying away, the villager meticulously complied. He returned to the monk the next day.

"Monk," he said and smiled, "I have obeyed your instruction exactly. What should I do now?"

"Now?" "Now," intoned the monk, "go pick up every feather."

"But, but..." spluttered the villager, "it has been an entire night. This task is impossible!"

The monk nodded in agreement, turned and walked away.

The monk's response of walking away without further instruction suggests that the villager's realization of the impossibility of the task serves as a lesson in itself. It implies that true penance does not lie in completing an external task but in *internal reflection* and *transformation*.

The monk's response of instructing the villager to place feathers on every doorstep, and then asking them to pick them up the next day, highlights the consequences of the villager's actions. By scattering the feathers, the villager has spread negativity and discord throughout the community. The task of picking up the feathers becomes an impossible feat, underscoring the lingering effects and difficulties of undoing the harm caused by unkind words and hence the importance of compassion-filled communication.

In Chapter 6, we discuss the importance of compassionate communication in coaching and how it contributes to the client achieving headway. We look at techniques for empathetic listening and non-judgemental feedback to dissolve resistance into self-discovery and consequently enable clients to rewrite their narratives.

We shall experience how compassionate communication can become the catalyst for metamorphosis. Like an alchemist, the coach harnesses the power of empathy to transmute pain into healing, fear into courage, and limitation into boundless potential. We will discover the transformative art of holding space, where unconditional acceptance creates a fertile ground for uncovering one's identity and potential, so that clients delve into the depths of their being, shedding layers of self-doubt and finding their truth.

The wisdom of the Buddha reminds us to approach clients with loving-kindness, patience and unconditional positive regard through numerous examples:

1. **The Simile of the Saw**: Buddha compared one's harsh speech to being struck by a saw, thus stressing the harmful effects of using hurtful words. He encouraged practitioners to speak words that are comforting, helpful and uplifting, and promote accord and understanding.

   The Simile of the Saw, or the *Kakacupama Sutta*, is a teaching found in the *Majjhima Nikaya*, one of the collections of discourses in the *Pali Canon*, the ancient scriptures of Theravāda Buddhism. The *Majjhima Nikaya* is a compilation of Buddha's discourses which were delivered to his disciples during his lifetime. This discourse takes place in Savatthi, one of the major cities in ancient India, where the Buddha delivered teachings to his monastic community.

The Simile of the Saw serves as a timeless teaching that continues to be studied and reflected upon by Buddhists and practitioners of compassionate communication worldwide.[32]

2. **The Story of Angulimala**: Buddha encountered a notorious murderer named Angulimala who was feared by everyone. Instead of responding with anger or judgement, the Buddha approached him with compassion and saw his potential for goodness. Through patient dialogue brimming with affection and wise communication, Buddha helped Angulimala change his violent ways and attain enlightenment.[33]

3. The *Metta Sutta*: Buddha's discourse on loving-kindness, known as the *Metta Sutta*, teaches the importance of cultivating a boundless and all-encompassing love for all beings. This teaching promotes compassionate communication by inspiring practitioners to speak words that are thoughtful, soothing, and beneficial, thus developing goodwill and compassion towards others.[34]

4. **The Discourse on Right Speech**: Buddha included right speech as one of the aspects of **The Noble Eightfold Path**. He taught that our words should be honest, gentle, positive, and spoken at the right time. By practising the right speech, we cultivate compassionate communication that avoids gossip, harsh speech, and divisive language.

These examples from Buddha's teachings highlight the importance of the power of words.

Can compassionate communication rewire neural pathways and dissolve limiting beliefs? Yes, numerous studies have demonstrated the positive effects of compassionate communication on brain structure and function. For example, research conducted by Tania Singer and her colleagues at the Max Planck Institute for Human Cognitive and Brain Sciences found that engaging in compassionate communication activates brain regions associated with empathy, understanding and emotional regulation.[35] This suggests that practising compassion can boost neural connections related to empathy and emotional well-being.

Furthermore, a study published in the *Journal of Experimental Social Psychology* by Breines and Chen (2012) showed that hearing compassionate words from others can reduce stress and improve psychological well-being. Participants who received compassionate messages experienced a decrease in cortisol levels, which indicates a reduction in stress response.[36]

Consider a coaching scenario where a client holds the belief that he is not capable of succeeding in his career. Through compassionate communication, the coach can challenge and reframe this belief.

When the coach extends support, encouragement, and an ability to look at alternative perspectives, it triggers the release of oxytocin, often referred to as the *bonding hormone*. Oxytocin augments feelings of trust, connection and well-being. It promotes a sense of safety and openness, which allows the client to engage in deeper self-reflection.

The coach might say:

"Let's explore your belief that you're not capable of succeeding in your career. Can we take a closer look at your accomplishments so far? Often, our perception can be coloured by specific experiences. What strengths and skills have you demonstrated in your career so far?"

The coach can help shift the client's perspective from self-doubt to self-confidence.

Neuroplasticity, the brain's ability to change and adapt, plays a crucial role in rewiring neural pathways. When the client consistently receives positive and empowering messages through compassionate communication, it triggers neuroplastic changes in the brain. These changes involve the formation of new neural connections and the strengthening of existing ones, gradually rewiring the brain's default response from negativity to empowerment, which can lead to a shift in beliefs and behaviours.

What is Neuroplasticity?

It is the brain's remarkable ability to reorganize itself by forming new neural connections throughout life. It is the foundation of learning, memory and adaptation. Here are some key points about neuroplasticity:

Definition: Neuroplasticity refers to the brain's capacity to change its structure and function in response to experiences, learning and environmental influences.

Neural Connections: The brain consists of billions of neurons that communicate through intricate networks of connections called *synapses*. Neuroplasticity allows the brain to modify existing connections, create new ones and reorganize its networks.

Experience-dependent Plasticity: Neuroplasticity is driven by experiences and learning. When we engage in new activities, acquire new skills or learn new information, the brain undergoes structural and functional changes to support those processes.

Hebbian Plasticity: This is a foundational principle of neuroplasticity, often summarized as *cells that fire together wire together*. When neurons are repeatedly activated in synchrony, the connections between them strengthen, facilitating faster and more efficient communication.

Synaptic Pruning: Neuroplasticity also involves the elimination of unused or less active synapses. Through a process called *synaptic pruning*, the brain refines its neural connections and discards unnecessary or inefficient ones to optimize its functioning.

Lifelong Plasticity: While neuroplasticity is most pronounced during early development, it continues throughout life. The adult brain retains the capacity to adjust and alter in response to new experiences, learning and environmental demands.

Therapeutic Applications: Understanding neuroplasticity has implications for various fields, including cognitive rehabilitation, psychotherapy and coaching. By leveraging neuroplasticity, interventions can be designed to promote positive changes, overcome limitations and improve well-being.[37]

When the client feels understood, supported and accepted, it reduces the activation of the amygdala, the brain's fear centre. This deactivation lowers stress levels and allows the client to approach challenges with greater clarity and resilience.

By utilizing compassionate communication techniques, the coach not only fosters a growth-oriented coaching relationship but also taps into the neurobiological mechanisms that bring about a desired change.

In addition to the neural mechanisms discussed earlier, compassionate communication also engages processes, such as *mirror neurons, cognitive reappraisal,* and *emotion regulation*!

Mirror neurons are a fascinating aspect of our brain's functioning. They are specialized cells that fire not only when we perform an action but also when we observe someone else performing the same action. This mirroring effect allows us to connect with others and appreciate their experiences on a deeper level. When a coach demonstrates empathy and compassion through their communication, mirror neurons in the client's brain are activated, leading to heartfelt interactions.

Cognitive reappraisal is another important process influenced by compassionate communication. It involves reinterpreting and reframing the meaning of a situation or experience. Through compassionate communication, the coach helps the client reframe his self-doubt and limiting beliefs, as well as encourages a more positive and empowering interpretation of his experiences. This cognitive reapprasial process can lead to a shift in the client's outlook and viewpoints.

Emotion regulation is also bettered through compassionate communication. By acknowledging and validating the client's emotions, the coach helps the client develop emotion regulation skills. This includes identifying and understanding their emotions, managing emotional reactions and finding healthy ways to cope with trying situations. As the client becomes more adept at regulating their emotions, they can deal with obstacles and setbacks with a stronger will and grit.

By incorporating these processes, compassionate communication taps into the intricate workings of the brain. It influences how we perceive and interpret experiences, how we connect with others on an empathic level and how we regulate our emotions and can catalyse a lasting change in clients' lives that they have been hoping for.

Here is a fictional case study of a big business firm highlighting the application of compassionate communication:

Client: ABC Corporation

Objective: Enhancing Interdepartmental Collaboration and Communication

Background:

ABC Corporation, a multinational company with various departments, experienced hurdles in interdepartmental collaboration and communication. Silos and miscommunication led to inefficiencies and hindered the company's overall performance. The leadership team sought external coaching support to address these issues and infuse a spirit of cooperation and alliance amongst teams.

Coaching Approach:

The coaching intervention focused on cultivating compassionate communication practices to bridge the gaps between departments and increase collaboration throughout the organization.

1. **Individual Coaching Sessions:**

   Coaches conducted individual coaching sessions with employees to understand their communication challenges and develop strategies to build empathy and tolerance. Through *deep listening* and *powerful questioning*, coaches helped individuals look into their communication patterns and identify opportunities for betterment.

2. **Team Coaching Workshops:**

   Coaches facilitated team coaching workshops where participants engaged in experiential exercises and discussions to further empathy, active listening, and effective communication skills. The workshops provided a safe space for teams to address conflicts, understand different perspectives, and find shared solutions.

3. **Peer-to-peer Coaching Circles:**

   Employees were encouraged to form peer-to-peer coaching circles, where they could support and coach each other in strengthening their communication skills. These circles provided a platform for practising active listening, giving constructive feedback, and building trust among colleagues.

4. **Goal Setting and Accountability:**

   Coaches helped individuals and teams set communication-related goals that aligned with the organization's vision and values. They provided ongoing assistance and accountability to ensure that these goals were being actively pursued and progress was being made.

Results:

The coaching intervention resulted in significant improvements in interdepartmental collaboration and communication at ABC Corporation. Employees developed a greater consideration of each other's perspectives, which led to improved cooperation, trust, and shared problem-solving. The cultivation of compassionate communication practices created an upbeat and inclusive work environment, leading to creativity and innovation. Over time, silos were broken down, and employees demonstrated a greater willingness to share knowledge and back each other across departments. This resulted in increased efficiency, better decision-making and improved overall performance for the company.

You may think, could something stand in the way of the above?

If yes, then what are those possible roadblocks?

Here are some of the common barriers to compassionate communication and popular strategies to overcome them:

1. **Lack of self-awareness**: One barrier to compassionate communication is a lack of self-awareness, which can prevent us from recognizing our truths. To overcome this, we can practice emotional intelligence exercises to develop a deeper understanding of ourselves.

   Some emotional intelligence (EI) exercises that align with compassionate communication are given below:

   a) **Emotional Audit**: Conduct a regular emotional audit by reflecting on your emotions and their underlying causes. Take time to recognize and affirm your emotions, both positive and negative without judgement. This exercise promotes self-awareness and understanding of your emotional patterns.

   b) **Reappraise**: Practice cognitive restructuring, which involves reframing and reinterpreting demanding situations in a more positive and constructive light. When faced with a difficult emotion or scenario consciously contest negative thoughts and find alternative perspectives. This exercise helps in managing and regulating emotions effectively.

   c) **Replenish:** Prioritize self-care activities that replenish your emotional well-being. Engage in activities that bring you joy, relaxation, and peace, such as hobbies, exercise, mindfulness, or spending time in nature. These help in managing stress, rejuvenating the energy levels and maintaining emotional balance. By incorporating these exercises into your routine, you can enhance your well-being.

d) **Emotional reactivity**: When we are emotionally reactive, it can be daunting to respond compassionately in communication. Some methods to overcome this barrier include practising emotional regulation techniques, such as deep breathing, taking a pause before responding, consciously choosing empathy, and understanding over-reactive behaviour.

Emotional Regulation Techniques:

Practising PAUSE:

The acronym **PAUSE** is a helpful technique for developing **emotional intelligence** (EI) skills. Each letter represents a key aspect of the practice:

P—Pause: Take a moment to pause and step back from a situation when you notice strong emotions arising. This allows you to be more self-aware and practise self-regulation.

A—Assess: Assess and identify your emotions. Pay attention to how you are feeling and try to understand the underlying reasons behind those emotions. This helps you gain clarity about your internal state.

U—Understand: Seek to understand the emotions of others involved in the situation. Practice empathy by putting yourself in their shoes and considering their perspective and feelings.

S—Strategize: Adopt strategies to manage emotions effectively. Try out healthy coping mechanisms, problem-solving techniques or communication skills that can help you be more in control of eventualities.

E—Engage: Engage in thoughtful and constructive communication. Use your understanding of emotions, both yours and others, to partake in respectful and empathetic dialogue to build better relationships and resolve conflicts.

The PAUSE technique empowers individuals to be more mindful and intentional in their emotional responses. It can be effectively used with clients during coaching by supporting them in practising these.[38]

2. **Mastering Inner Silence**

    To cultivate inner silence, there are various practices and activities that can help us settle down and find stillness within. One approach is to schedule regular power pauses.

The Power Pause

Practice the power pause by scheduling 1–2-minute breaks every hour. Pauses may happen during natural transitions, such as working at home, in between meetings or calls, upon rising or just before bed. By setting an alarm on our phones to remind us, we can create intentional moments of quiet reflection.

Once you get to know inner silence, you will want nothing else but to live in that space all the time.

The Power Pause Practice:

♦   Find a place to sit, place your feet on the floor and your hand on your thighs, and close your eyes.

♦   For a moment, bring your attention way down to your feet. Just notice your feet on the ground, your seat in the chair and your hands on your legs.

♦   Now, focus on your heart which is beating. Find your pulse somewhere in your body. Bring your mind and your attention to your body as quickly as possible.

- Now place light attention on the natural rhythm of your breath. With your mind resting on your breath, you may start to notice a sense of ease; notice, as you exhale fully, that there is less tension and noise.

- For the next few moments notice your feet, hands, heartbeat, and breath or wherever your attention lands on any one of those areas in your body—which is just perfect—a perfect way to take a pause.

Now, open your eyes if they have been closed and just notice what a few moments of pause can do. Our bodies are magnificent and brilliant stabilizing systems when we give our bodies and our minds the opportunity to slow down.

Benefits of the Power Pause:

- Allows your body and mind to balance and align.

- Cultivates a sense of inner calm and tranquillity.

- Enhances overall well-being and mental clarity.

To summarise, taking regular power pauses throughout the day can help you find inner silence and create moments of stillness. By directing your attention to your physical sensations, heartbeat and breath, you can experience a sense of ease and quiet reflection. These pauses allow your body and mind to reset. [39]

Introducing Power Pauses in Coaching Sessions:

Coaches can guide clients to practice power pauses during coaching sessions to ground themselves and expand their self-awareness. By inviting clients to pause, coaches make room for clients to centre themselves, release tension and allow a sense of calm and ease to descend.

Further, they can egg them on to take a pause whenever they encounter moments of stress, overwhelm or uncertainty. This helps clients regulate their nervous system, reduce reactivity, and access a more grounded state.

3. **Assumptions and Judgements:** Making assumptions and judgements about others can hinder compassionate communication. To overcome this barrier, we can have a mindset of curiosity and openness, thus seeking to understand others' standpoints without jumping to conclusions. As discussed, active listening, asking clarifying questions and suspending judgement can help in this process.

Some examples of clarifying questions are:

a) Can you please provide more details or examples to help me understand your viewpoint better?

b) Could you clarify what you meant when you mentioned [specific term or concept]?

c) Can you elaborate on how that situation made you feel and why it had that impact on you?

4. **Lack of Empathy:** Empathy is an elemental aspect of compassionate communication. If we struggle to empathize with others, it can hinder effective communication.

Here is an example to illustrate some significant ways, such as perspective-taking and reflective paraphrasing to build empathy:

Team Leader: Mei-Ling

Team Member: Hiroshi

Mei-Ling: "Hiroshi, I've noticed that your recent work hasn't been meeting our expectations. Can we talk about what might be going on?"

Hiroshi: "I've been feeling overwhelmed and demotivated lately. I'm struggling to balance my workload and personal problems."

Mei-Ling (perspective-taking): "It sounds like you've been experiencing a lot of pressure both at work and in your personal life. I can understand how that could affect your performance and motivation."

Hiroshi: "Yes, exactly. It's been perplexing to focus and stay productive."

Mei-Ling (reflective paraphrasing): "So, it seems like the combination of work demands and personal adversities has made it difficult for you to concentrate and maintain productivity."

In this example, representing an Asian cultural context, Mei-Ling engages in a conversation that applies *perspective-taking* and *reflective paraphrasing* to understand and empathize with Hiroshi's dilemmas.

5. **Communication Style and Language**: Certain communication styles or language choices may unintentionally hinder compassionate communication. Developing effective communication skills, such as active listening, using **I** statements, and seeking common ground can help overcome this barrier.

Here is an example of a dialogue showcasing the development of effective communication skills:

Person A: "I've noticed that we've been having some communication issues lately. I feel like we're not really understanding each other. Can we talk about it?"

Person B: "Yes, I've noticed that too. Sometimes, I feel like my opinions are not being heard."

Person A (active listening): "I hear you saying that you feel unheard. Can you give me an example of when you felt that way?"

Person B: "Well, during our team meeting yesterday, I shared my ideas, but it seemed like everyone just brushed them off without really considering them."

Person A (seeking common ground): "I understand how that can be frustrating. I've also felt like my ideas haven't been given enough attention in the past."

Person B: "Exactly! It's like we're not valuing each other's perspectives."

Person A (using I statements): "I want us to work together more effectively, and I believe, that starts with improving our communication. I'm committed to actively listening to your ideas and finding common ground."

Person B: "That sounds good to me. I'm willing to do the same."

In this dialogue, Person A and Person B are addressing their communication issues by applying active listening, using **I** statements, and seeking common ground. They build a foundation for open and effective communication, thus allowing them to find solutions and improve their understanding of one another.

Let us compare the dialogue above—using I statements and seeking common ground with a conversed dialogue:

Hypothetical dialogue (using *You* statements):

Person A: *"You never listen to me. You always dismiss my ideas."*

Person B: *"Well, you never consider other perspectives. You're always so stubborn."*

In this hypothetical dialogue, the use of *you* statements creates a blame-oriented and confrontational tone. It can escalate tensions and trigger defensive responses, thus hindering effective communication and problem-solving. Each person is fixated on criticizing the other's behaviour rather than seeking to understand or find common ground.

On the other hand, the examples using the *I* statement bolster a more constructive and collaborative mood. This approach allows for the acknowledgement of individual perspectives and nudges both parties to work together towards a resolution.

In conclusion, using *I* statements promotes ownership of one's feelings and experiences, thus reducing defensiveness, which increases the likelihood of finding mutually beneficial solutions.

6. **Lack of Trust and Safety**: When there is a lack of trust or psychological safety in a communication environment, it can impede compassionate communication. Building trust and creating a safe space for open dialogue requires actively listening and honouring confidentiality amongst others.

Here is a brilliant real-life example to illustrate the impact of psychological safety:

A study conducted by Google called *Project Aristotle* examined hundreds of teams within the company to determine the factors that contribute to team effectiveness. The study found that the most successful teams shared one common characteristic—psychological safety.[40]

Teams with high levels of psychological safety had members who felt comfortable speaking up, sharing their ideas and taking risks without the fear of being judged or punished. These teams experienced higher levels of creativity, innovation and problem-solving. They were also more likely to meet their goals and achieve better performance.

Additionally, research by Amy Edmondson, a professor at Harvard Business School has shown that organizations with a strong culture of psychological safety have higher employee engagement and increased productivity.[41]

These examples highlight the tangible benefits of psychological safety in a corporate environment, thus demonstrating its great impact on team dynamics, innovation and overall organizational success.

By taking into account these barriers, we have the power to cultivate an environment where compassionate communication thrives, nurturing genuine bonds with those around us.

Non-judgemental Feedback and its Impassioned Role in Compassionate Communication:

It is important to look at non-judgemental feedback, as it is an essential component of compassionate communication. It is a type of constructive feedback that centres on sharing objective observations, specific insights, and suggestions for improvement without attaching personal judgement or criticism. It stresses the behaviour or performance rather than the individual.

An example of a modern leader known for practising non-judgemental feedback is Satya Nadella, the CEO of Microsoft. Nadella is known for his empathetic and inclusive leadership style, which spotlights building a culture of psychological safety and a growth mindset. He champions open dialogue, values diverse perspectives, and gives feedback in a non-judgemental manner, thus giving attention to learning and development rather than blame or criticism. His approach nurtures a setting where employees feel valued and empowered to take risks and innovate.

When conveying non-judgemental feedback, it is important to follow these techniques:

a) **Stick to observations**: Focus on specific behaviours or actions that you have witnessed. Avoid arriving at wrongly placed conclusions or making unfounded interpretations. Steer away from explanations that lack factual or logical support and are merely speculative in nature. For instance, instead of saying, "You always interrupt others," say, "I noticed that you spoke while others were still sharing their ideas during our meeting."

b) **Highlight impact**: Describe the impact of the person's behaviour or actions on yourself or others. Explain how it made you feel or the consequences it had. For instance, say, "When you arrived late to the meeting, it caused delays and disrupted the flow of the discussion."

c) **Provide suggestions**: Instead of zeroing in solely on the negatives, present constructive suggestions for improvement. Propose alternatives or strategies that can help amplify their performance. For example, say, "To elevate your communication skills, you could try using more open-ended questions to inspire dialogue and engagement."

d) **Facilitate a supportive environment**: Reiterate that your input is geared towards aiding their advancement. Allow people to say that they made a mistake, need help or clarity to move ahead. Encourage open dialogue, active listening, and an understanding that constructive feedback is a stepping-stone towards improvement.

Benefits of non-judgemental feedback that have been widely observed and reported:

1. **Increased employee engagement**: Non-judgemental feedback has been linked to higher levels of employee engagement. Employees are more likely to be motivated and committed to their work.

2. **Enhanced performance and productivity**: Non-judgemental feedback helps individuals concentrate on specific behaviours and areas for improvement rather than personal criticism. This allows for targeted development and skill enhancement, thus leading to more productivity.

3. **Strengthened self-awareness and growth mindset**: Non-judgemental feedback ennobles a growth mindset and welcomes opportunities for learning and development. By providing specific observations and recommendations for betterment without harsh judgement, individuals are more likely to reflect on their performance and actively seek ways to build their skills.

4. **Improved relationships and trust**: Non-judgemental feedback is co-linked with healthier and trusting relationships. When feedback is delivered in a compassionate and constructive manner, it strengthens ties between team members, leaders and employees, thus leading to better partnership and teamwork.

It is important to remember that crafting a feedback-rich culture and ensuring effective feedback practices are essential for reaping these benefits.

In this search, we delved into the untouched potential of compassionate communication not only in coaching but in the wider world and its intense impact on any individual, organisation and yes, on client growth and transformation. When coaches are attuned to the unspoken, magic can happen. This ground-breaking approach builds heart-to-heart bonds between the coach and the client. Let us all take a pioneering step in our coaching practice [and continue if we are already doing so, which I believe most of you are] and reveal its unparalleled capacity to bring forth the latent possibilities within every client.

Conclusion:

This chapter, "The Sublime Conversations" underscores the unerasable effect of compassionate communication in coaching. Through its inquiry into empathy, active listening, and open dialogue, the chapter reveals how words become catalysts for change. With relatable examples, we are shown the intricacies of building trust, fuelling growth, and sparking positive shifts. We learn that when communication is grounded in compassion, it becomes the foundation of effective coaching.

> *Speak only endearing speech, speech that is welcomed. Speech, when it brings no evil to others, is a pleasant thing.*

> – Buddha

Breaking Free from Limiting Beliefs

An Often-heard Story About Limiting Beliefs

The first trick an elephant trainer trains an elephant to do is not to escape. When the elephant is still but a baby, the trainer chains the infant's leg to a huge log. When/if the elephant tries to escape, the log proves to be stronger, and he gives up. Eventually, the elephant becomes so used to its captivity, that even when it has grown huge and strong, all the trainer merely has to do is tie the chain around the elephant's leg to anything—even a tiny little twig—and the elephant will not even try to escape.

It has become a prisoner of its past—a prisoner of its limiting beliefs.

This elephant and its twig are a lot like you and the pain, struggles and limitations of your past.

Nothing in your past is in your present now.

In Chapter 7, we shift our focus to the role of the compassionate coach in supporting clients to challenge their limiting beliefs and move past onto a promising future.

We examine how the concept of impermanence in Buddhism can help clients question and surpass their fixed beliefs and attachments while looking at things in a fresh manner and seeing and appreciating new possibilities. We also learn how to hold a space of possibility and potential for our clients, fully convinced of their innate capacity to flourish.

We introduce coaching techniques to defy limiting beliefs. We once again draw attention to the role of compassion in this process, as clients circumnavigate their fears and insecurities to live more purposefully.

In Buddhism, the principle of impermanence, or **anicca** teaches us that everything in life is in a constant state of change. This philosophy resonates strongly with today's dynamic work environment, where organizations and individuals must learn to be agile.

Within the context of the book, we learn how acknowledging the ever-changing nature of circumstances, concerns, and even our thoughts and emotions, can lead to a more adaptable mindset. Recognizing impermanence allows us to release attachments to rigid expectations or resistance to change, thus bestowing us with greater flexibility and an ability to think more creatively. By integrating the concept of impermanence into coaching practices, coaches can help clients develop resilience and a proactive outlook. This involves viewing setbacks as learning opportunities and finding meaning and value in the present moment.

Limiting Beliefs

First, it is important to understand what are limiting beliefs.

Let us do that through some common life examples:

"I'm not smart enough": This limiting belief often stems from past experiences or negative feedback that makes an individual doubt his acumen. It can gravely impede individual and career development, thus inhibiting the pursuit of novel ventures and tackling intellectually demanding endeavours with confidence.

"I'm not worthy of success": This belief is rooted in a past experience of failure leading to feelings of inadequacy and low self-esteem. It can create self-sabotaging behaviours, inhibitions, and reluctance which can hinder individuals from fully fathoming their potential and capitalizing on opportunities for progress.

"I don't deserve love": This limiting belief can be a result of past traumas or experiences of rejection, making individuals question their worthiness of love and healthy relationships. It can impact their ability to form meaningful connections and maintain fulfilling partnerships.

"Success and happiness are only for others": This limiting belief is entrenched in unhealthy comparison and feelings of inadequacy. Individuals with this belief may think that others are more deserving or inherently luckier, thus leading them to doubt the possibility of their success and happiness. It can create a sense of resignation and deter individuals from pursuing their goals with confidence and resilience.

"I can't change": This limiting belief suggests a fixed mindset, where individuals believe that their abilities, behaviours or circumstances are unchangeable. It obstructs individuals from moving forward, mars the ability to spot fresh avenues or derive lessons from setbacks and attain favourable amends in life.

These examples illustrate how limiting beliefs can hold individuals back.

Identifying and braving these beliefs is a crucial step towards forward and upward movement in life.

However, letting go of limiting beliefs and making room for growth is indeed easier said than done, especially when dealing with emotional challenges like feeling down or depressed. In our book, we understand and acknowledge the complexity of the human experience, and we offer tangible and compassionate approaches to support readers in their journey.

Let's scour through each one:

"I'm not smart enough":

- Start small and focus on one area of learning or skill development at a time.

- Celebrate even the tiniest progress to reinforce self-confidence and motivation.

- Seek support from mentors, friends or coaches who can provide direction and cheer you on.

"I'm not worthy of success":

♦ Practice self-compassion during moments of self-doubt, thus acknowledging that it is okay to struggle.

♦ Habituate yourself to make daily affirmations or engage in positive self-talk to defeat negative beliefs.

♦ Have a self-care routine that includes activities that bring joy and relaxation.

"I don't deserve love":

♦ Seek professional support if needed to address past traumas and work through emotional pain.

♦ Practice self-soothing techniques during difficult emotions, such as deep breathing or grounding exercises.

♦ Engage in activities that promote self-love and acceptance, such as journaling or self-reflection.

"Success and happiness are only for others":

♦ Focus on your unique strengths and accomplishments, thus valuing your individual journey.

♦ Limit exposure to social media or other triggers that may fuel comparison.

♦ Surround yourself with a supportive community that commends your progress.

"I can't change":

♦ Start by acknowledging your emotions and seeking help if you are struggling with depression or low mood.

♦ Set realistic and achievable goals that honour your current emotional state.

♦ Celebrate the courage and effort you put into trying, even if progress is slow.

In this book, we prioritize sensitivity to the emotional challenges that people face and offer some antidotes. Our aim is to help readers feel succoured in their journey towards emotional well-being.

Here are some coaching techniques that can be effective in challenging limiting beliefs and supporting individuals in overcoming them.

Socratic Questioning: Get the clients to challenge the truth behind underlying assumptions and evidence that underpin their limiting beliefs through thought-provoking questions. Employ open-ended inquiries to disrupt their thinking and redirect them towards alternate possibilities.

Here's how you can apply it:

a) **Identify the belief**: Start by identifying the limiting belief. For example, "I'm not good enough."

b) **Question assumptions**: Ask questions that challenge the assumptions behind the belief. For instance, "What evidence supports this belief? Are there instances when you have succeeded?"

c) **Seek alternatives**: Encourage exploring alternative perspectives. Ask, "What might be a more balanced way to view this situation? Can you think of times when you've achieved something similar?"

d) **Evidence and proof**: Ask for concrete evidence that supports the belief. For example, "Can you provide specific instances where this belief has been true? Is there any evidence that contradicts this belief?"

e) **Consequences**: Explore the consequences of holding onto this belief. Ask, "How does this belief impact your decisions and actions? What might you miss out on due to this belief?"

f) **Reality testing**: Encourage testing the validity of the belief. Ask, "What would happen if you acted as though this belief were not true? How could you find out if it's accurate or not?"

g) Reframe and replace: Help reframe the belief by asking, "What's a more empowering way to think about yourself? What strengths and qualities do you possess?"

h) Meta-questioning: Encourage self-awareness by asking, "Why do you think you adopted this belief? Could it be influenced by past experiences?"

i) Reflect on origin: Ask questions like, "Where did this belief come from? Is it your original thought, or was it influenced by someone else?"

j) Future possibilities: Shift the focus to positive outcomes. Ask, "What could you achieve if you let go of this belief? How might your life improve?"

Remember, Socratic questioning is about guiding someone's thinking, not imposing your own beliefs. It's a gradual process that helps individuals arrive at more rational and empowering perspectives by assessing their suppositions.

1. **Cognitive Shift**: Facilitate clients in reframing limiting beliefs, thus transforming them into growth-oriented thoughts. Inspire viewing challenges as opportunities and past failures as valuable learning lessons.

Here's how:

Coach: "How can you reframe the thought, 'I might not be qualified for this promotion' into a more empowering belief?"

Client: "I can shift it to 'I have the skills and experience needed for this role, and I am prepared to take on new challenges.'"

2. **Visualization and Affirmations**: Guide clients to visualize their desired outcomes and create positive affirmations that counter negative beliefs. Urge regular repetition to reinforce empowering beliefs.

Here's how:

Coach: "Imagine yourself confidently leading a team meeting. What positive affirmations can support your confidence?"

Client: "I would say, 'I am a competent leader, and my insights and contributions are valuable to the team.'"

3. **Evidence-based Perspective**: Help clients collect evidence from their experiences that challenge their limiting beliefs. Identify instances of success, resilience and strength to build confidence.

Here's how:

Coach: *"Think about a recent accomplishment that showcases your abilities. How does that evidence contradict your self-doubt?"*

Client: *"I recently received praise from a colleague for my problem-solving skills, which shows I have the ability to excel."*

4. **Behaviour Rehearsal**: Support clients in practising new behaviours that are aligned with empowering beliefs. Role-play challenging scenarios and guide them to adopt constructive responses.

Here's how:

Coach: *"Let's role-play a networking scenario where you typically feel uncertain. How can you approach it differently?"*

Client: *"In this scenario, I can focus on asking open-ended questions and actively listening, thus showcasing my genuine interest in others."*

5. **Goal Accountability**: Assist clients in setting realistic goals that push them beyond their limiting beliefs. Offer ongoing support and encouragement to keep them on track toward growth and achievement.

Here's how:

Coach: *"What is a goal that challenges your belief and pushes you outside your comfort zone?"*

Client: *"I want to volunteer for a leadership role in a project to prove to myself that I can handle responsibilities."*

Ultimately, understanding the impermanence of situations and utilization of the coaching techniques outlined above can speak to the needs of the modern workplace. By encouraging employees to courageously welcome change, conquer self-doubt and envision success, organizations can promote a culture that upholds growth, innovation, and resilience.

Here are a few examples of how organisations can do so:

1. Adapting to Change: Building Nimble Organizations

In a rapidly evolving business landscape, organizations must innovate and acclimatize to stay competitive. Recognizing the transitoriness of market trends, customer preferences and technology allows leaders to proactively take on change, adjust strategies, and seize new opportunities.

The Power of Nimble Leadership in Driving Organizational Success

Nimble organizations are masters at turning ideas into reality. Take the example of W.L. Gore, a company founded with the vision of furthering self-fulfilment and magnifying individual capabilities.[42]

In 1958, Wilbert Gore and his wife, Genevieve started an insulated cable company, W.L. Gore, from the basement of their Delaware home. Sixty years later, the basement business has grown into a multinational (but still privately owned) corporation with products used to power cities and space suits. At its core, this cultural principle is based on freedom—not to do whatever employees want but to help each other grow as leaders.

To create a nimble organization, three types of leaders play crucial roles: *entrepreneurial, enabling,* and *architecting.*

Entrepreneurial leaders are idea generators who inspire trust through expertise and reputation. They form adaptive teams that bridge boundaries, connect with stakeholders and coordinate tasks to bring ideas to life.

Enabling leaders, positioned in the middle of the hierarchy, support entrepreneurial leaders by removing obstacles and connecting like-minded groups. They coach employees through thought-provoking questions, endorsing a culture of ownership and collaboration.

Architecting leaders, at the top level, shape the organization's culture, structure and strategic priorities. They bring purpose off the wall and into daily decision-making, thus ensuring that everyone works in unison while empowering employees to engage in sensemaking with customers and frontline employees.

Nimble leadership creates an environment where employees feel enabled, equipped, and backed to lead and innovate. Instead of a command-and-control approach, nimble organizations value dialogue, safety and alignment with culture and policy.

By adopting agile leadership principles, organizations can unlock the full capabilities of their workforce and capitalize on emerging prospects and secure a competitive advantage.[43]

Thus, in today's time, anticipating and understanding impermanence and shedding limiting beliefs are the key. By espousing nimble organizations and holding nimble leadership principles, leaders can churn out success stories. This stance values *collaboration* and *purpose-driven alignment*.

2. Bouncing Back in Uncertainty: Strengthening Organizational Resilience

The term resilience was introduced into the English language in the early 17th century from the Latin verb, *resilire,* meaning *to rebound* or *recoil.*

Uncertainty is a constant in today's work environment. Taking it into account helps individuals develop resilience by accepting that circumstances will change, setbacks are only temporary, and breakthroughs can happen. This outlook positions employees in a way that is advantageous to bounce back from holdups more effectively.

Some tangible and proven data on strengthening organizational resilience are:

A) **Robust Financial Performance**: Companies that prioritize resilience tend to achieve about 47% higher return on assets (ROA) and outperform industry peers in terms of financial stability, as per McKinsey and Company.[44]

B) **Engaged Workforce and Talent Retention**: Gallup reports that resilient organizations have almost 21% higher employee engagement and significantly lower turnover rates compared to those with lower resilience.[45]

C) **Agile Decision-making**: Deloitte's survey indicates that resilient organizations exhibit faster and more agile decision-making, according to around 94% of executives.[46]

D) **Customer Trust and Loyalty**: Resilient companies enjoy higher levels of customer trust and loyalty, with 74% of customers stating that they are more likely to remain loyal during times of crisis, according to the Edelman Trust Barometer.[47]

E) **Adaptability to Market Changes**: Resilient organizations have a greater ability to respond and adapt to market disruptions, thus resulting in a 26% higher survival rate during challenging economic periods, as highlighted in the Journal of Business Research.[48]

It is important to keep in mind that these findings are based on general research and may vary depending on industry-specific factors and individual organizational contexts.

So, we see that by accepting impermanence, leaders foster a culture that thrives in uncertainty, retains talent and builds trust. Defeating self-imposed barriers becomes the foundation for fortitude and flexibility.

3. Embracing Innovation: Cultivating Blue-sky Thinking

Impermanence encourages a way of thinking that welcomes innovation and experimentation. Organizations that understand that current methods and practices may become outdated can promote a culture that values creativity, continuous learning and new ideas. This enables them to stay ahead of the curve and attune to emerging trends.

Here are the examples of companies embracing innovation and cultivating blue-sky thinking:

Google: Google is known for its 20%-time policy, where employees are encouraged to spend 20% of their work hours on projects of personal interest. This has resulted in several successful innovations, including Gmail, which now has over 1.5 billion users worldwide. Additionally, Google's innovation lab, Google X, has developed projects, such as self-driving cars and Project Loon, a network of high-altitude balloons that provide internet access to remote areas.

Tesla: Tesla's innovative approach to electric vehicles has disrupted the automotive industry. The company has achieved significant milestones, such as producing the Model S, which became the best-selling electric car worldwide in 2015. Tesla's commitment to innovation is reflected in its continuous advancements in battery technology, thus resulting in increased range and improved charging infrastructure.

Netflix: Netflix has transformed the entertainment industry by investing heavily in original content. In 2013, the company released its first critically acclaimed original series, *House of Cards*, which set the stage for its expansion into producing award-winning shows, such as *Stranger Things* and *The Crown*. Today, Netflix has over 200 million subscribers globally, thus demonstrating the success of its innovative content strategy.

Apple: Apple's focus on innovation and design has made it a leader in consumer electronics. The introduction of the iPhone revolutionized the smartphone market, with over two billion iPhones sold worldwide. Apple's App Store has also played a significant role in fostering innovation with developers creating over 2.2 million apps for users to enhance their Apple device experience.

Through their celebration of innovation and cultivation of visionary thinking, these companies exemplify an acute understanding of impermanence. By standing up to and surpassing beliefs that hold us back, they consistently break new ground, thus pushing the boundaries of what is possible and driving disruptive change.

Therefore, these companies' commitment to innovation and cultivating blue-sky thinking has not only led to remarkable products and services but also propelled them to become industry leaders with a powerful edge over competitors in the fast-paced market, which sets the stage for sustained success.

4. Fostering Agile Teams: Preparing for Disruption

Teams that welcome impermanence understand that roles and responsibilities may shift, projects may evolve, and individuals may come and go. This makes room for collaboration, flexibility and a willingness to learn from and appreciate different standpoints. Agile teams are better equipped to handle unexpected changes and maintain high performance.

Here are a few stories of agile transformation of well-known pioneers:

A) **Spotify**: Spotify implemented the ***Spotify Model*** as a framework for scaling agile practices. It organized teams into ***squads*** that were cross-functional and self-organizing, thus allowing for faster decision-making and innovation.

Squads formed ***tribes*** based on similar areas of focus, and ***chapters*** provided opportunities for knowledge-sharing and skill development. This model built a culture of collaboration, autonomy and continuous learning, thus enabling Spotify to adapt quickly to market changes.[49]

Impact achieved by highly successful¹ agile transformations

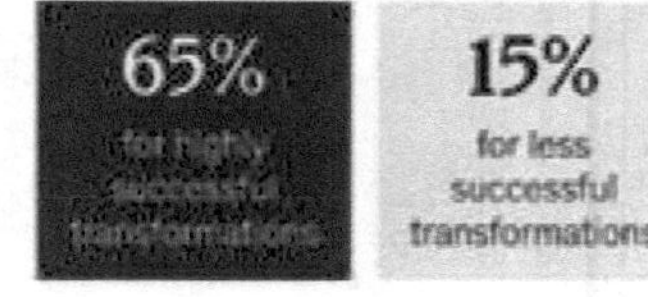

Source: McKinsey and Company

B) Amazon: Amazon adopted a decentralized and customer-centric approach to agile transformation. They organized teams around small, customer-focused units known as ***two-pizza teams***, which were empowered to make autonomous decisions. The company adopted an iterative development process and a culture of experimentation, thus encouraging employees to take calculated risks and learn from failures. This agile mindset allowed Amazon to deliver new features and services rapidly, continuously improve customer experiences and drive innovation.[50]

C) Zappos: Zappos implemented a holacratic organizational structure, thus replacing traditional hierarchies with self-organizing teams. It impressed upon employee autonomy, thus spurring individuals to take on multiple roles and make decisions collectively. Zappos also implemented agile practices, such as iterative development, continuous improvement and regular retrospectives to bolster its adaptability and responsiveness. This agile transformation brought in a culture of innovation, employee engagement and customer-centricity, which contributed to Zappos' success as a customer service-focused retailer.[51]

Iterative Development:

It is a process in which a project or product is continuously refined and improved through multiple, small cycles of development. Instead of trying to create a perfect solution all at once, iterative development allows for gradual progress and feedback-driven adjustments.

Here is an example to illustrate iterative development:

Suppose a software development team is tasked with creating a new mobile app. Instead of building the entire app from scratch in one go, they adopt an iterative approach. They start by developing a basic version of the app with its core features. They then release this version to a select group of users for testing and feedback.

Based on the feedback received, the team identifies areas for improvement and new features that users desire. They then work on the next iteration and incorporate the suggested changes, as well as add new functionalities. This process continues through several iterations—each time enhancing the app, based on user feedback and evolving market demands.

The benefit of iterative development is that it allows the team to address issues and make improvements incrementally, which leads to a more refined and user-friendly product. It also allows for greater flexibility in adapting to changing requirements and market conditions.

In summary, iterative development enables continuous learning and adaptation and ensures that the final product is more robust and aligned with user needs.

Visionary companies, such as Spotify, Amazon, Netflix, and Zappos disrupted conventional thinking in their agile journeys. They defied traditional norms, built agile cultures, and welcomed change as a stimulus for growth. By challenging the status quo, they boosted innovation, cooperation, and rapid decision-making. These trailblazers prove that by acknowledging that impermanence is a reality and letting go of the stories we tell ourselves about—who we are that hold us back from becoming who we are meant to be—we can fuel extraordinary organizational success in fluid times. They inspire us to venture into the unknown, fearlessly evolve and manifest all that ability that lies latent.

5. Finding Meaning and Purpose: Defining a Common Goal

Impermanence prompts individuals to reflect on the fleeting nature of life and work. This introspection can inspire a search for deeper meaning and purpose in one's career. By bringing into line personal values with professional goals, individuals can find greater contentment, motivation and satisfaction in their work.

Some examples of studies that support the relationship between finding meaning and purpose in work and positive outcomes are:

a) **Employee Engagement**: A Gallup survey found that employees who strongly agree that they have a sense of purpose at work are 4.4 times more likely to be engaged compared to those who do not. (Source: *State of the Global Workplace* report by Gallup.)[52]

b) **Job Satisfaction**: A study published in the *Journal of Business Ethics* found a positive correlation between meaningful work and job satisfaction amongst employees in various industries.[53]

c) **Productivity and Performance**: According to a research report by the University of Warwick, happy and engaged employees were found to be 12% more productive compared to their unhappy counterparts.[54]

d) **Retention and Loyalty**: A study conducted by the Corporate Leadership Council revealed that employees who find their work meaningful are 69% less likely to consider leaving their organization within the next year.[55]

While these examples illustrate the positive impact of finding meaning and purpose in work, they do not specifically focus on the role of impermanence. However, the concept of impermanence can serve as a reminder to individuals to reflect on their priorities and seek deeper satisfaction in their careers.

Ultimately, the examples presented above stand as resounding proof of the potency of comprehending and embracing impermanence and change. These instances of innovation, agility, and nimbleness are parallel narratives that underscore the very essence of impermanence—where established norms shift and new directions emerge.

The synergy between embracing change and coaching is profound; it's about leading individuals to harness the dynamism of their surroundings. Compassionate coaches play a pivotal role in aiding clients to leave behind that which does not serve them anymore and charge ahead. By utilising the concept of impermanence in Buddhism, coaches espouse clients to question the solidity of their beliefs and attachments clearing the path for fresh possibilities.

Research demonstrates that coaching interventions that blend mindfulness and acceptance-based approaches, including impermanence, lead to explicit and conclusive outcomes. Clients who receive coaching which is focused on impermanence report higher levels of self-compassion and improved self-awareness.

Through compassionate communication and skilful partnering, coaches support clients in examining their closely held attachments and beliefs. The data-driven evidence supports its powerful impact.

In conclusion, this chapter presents the transformative potency of fully accepting impermanence. This synergism guides clients to challenge attachments and embrace change, stimulating innovation and resilience akin to modern workplaces. As coaches champion this paradigm shift, they enable clients to deal with uncertainty, ushering in growth and success. This chapter continues to underscore the harmony between Buddhist principles and coaching, revealing their ability to propel individuals beyond limitations.

All conditioned things are impermanent—when one sees this with wisdom, one turns away from suffering.

– Buddha

Chapter 8

The Mindful Coach's Toolkit

A Zen Story on Mindfulness:

In a monastery, there lived a young monk named Koji who was known for his impatience and restless nature. One day, seeking guidance, he approached his master, Sensei.

"Sensei," Koji said, "I struggle with being mindful. My mind constantly wanders, and I find it challenging to stay present."

Sensei smiled and handed Koji a small, empty bottle. He instructed him to go to the nearby river and fill the bottle with water but with a condition—Koji must fill the bottle without any distractions or allowing his mind to wander.

Excited to prove himself, Koji rushed to the river with the bottle in hand. However, as he dipped the bottle into the water, his mind was filled with thoughts about the past and worries about the future. He kept losing focus.

Frustrated, Koji returned to Sensei, admitting his failure. Sensei smiled and said, "Koji, the practice of mindfulness is like holding the bottle. Just as you must focus on the present moment to fill the bottle with water, you must stay present to fill your life with mindfulness. It's not about the quantity but the quality of your presence."

In this Zen story, Koji's struggle with mindfulness mirrors the challenges many face in staying present. The analogy of the small bottle and the river depicts the crux of mindfulness. The task seems simple—fill the bottle with water. However, Koji's mind's wanderings depict how easily we get pulled into past regrets and future anxieties, missing the present moment.

By likening the practice of mindfulness to holding the bottle and focusing on the present, the master conveys that mindfulness isn't just about completing a task. It's about immersing ourselves fully in the present and resisting the distractions that pull us away. It is not about achieving a perfect state of attention but rather, engaging in the practice of bringing our awareness back to the present moment, again and again, with patience and compassion.

The lesson transcends the bottle and the river; it signifies that mindfulness isn't confined to any particular activity. Just as the bottle's content matters less than the quality of mindfulness applied to fill it, in life, the depth of our experiences is enriched when we infuse mindfulness into our actions, interactions, and daily existence.

In Chapter 8, we turn our attention to the concept of mindfulness, a central pillar of Buddhist philosophy. We look at mindfulness as a state of non-judgemental awareness and its significance in coaching.

We see its various ever-lasting benefits in increasing self-awareness, reducing stress and achieving a state of holistic well-being.

We learn practical techniques for integrating mindfulness meditation into our coaching sessions, such as guided visualizations and breath awareness exercises.

What is Mindfulness Meditation?

Imagine sitting in a beautiful garden and noticing the colours, smells, and sounds around you. You are fully engaged in the present moment and observing everything with curiosity and without judgement. That is mindfulness. It is about being aware of the present moment without being preoccupied by worries about the past or future.

Mindfulness meditation is the *intentional practice* of being fully present in the moment without attachment. It involves directing our attention to the present experience, and developing a heightened awareness of our thoughts, feelings and sensations as they arise and pass, including the surrounding environment. It involves recognizing and acknowledging them without getting caught up in them or letting them control us. Through this, we forge an attitude of acceptance and curiosity, thus allowing us to observe our inner and outer experiences with clarity.

We become more attuned to the present moment and better able to regulate our emotions. *To say, mindfulness fortifies a state of non-reactive awareness.*

Techniques

Mindfulness can be practised through various techniques, such as meditation, breath awareness, body scans, and mindful movement, which we will discuss further. It is an underlying aspect of many spiritual and contemplative traditions, including Buddhism, and has also gained significant recognition in fields, such as psychology, neuroscience, and workplace well-being.

Through the power of mindfulness, we can attain a greater sense of inner calm. It brings presence and equanimity to daily activities, thus refining the quality of life.

The blending of mindfulness and meditation practices in coaching conversations can take various forms, depending on the specific needs and preferences of the coach and client. Here are some instances and ways in which mindfulness and meditation can be brought into coaching:

1. **Setting the Tone**: At the beginning of a coaching session, coaches can guide clients through a brief meditation or mindfulness exercise to create a calm and present-moment-focused environment.

    a) **Meditation or Mindfulness Exercise**

    Example:

    - Take a deep breath in, feeling the air filling your lungs and exhale slowly, thus releasing any tension or distractions.

    - Now, gently close your eyes and bring your focus to the present moment.

- Notice the sensation of your feet firmly grounded on the floor. Feel the support of the chair beneath you.

- As you continue to breathe deeply and mindfully, let any thoughts or worries float away like passing clouds. Bring your awareness to the here and now and allow yourself to fully arrive in this moment.

- Take this time totally to acknowledge any emotion or sensation that you are experiencing without judgement. Simply observe them with curiosity and compassion.

- Now, envision a clear intention for our coaching session today. What do you hope to achieve? Picture yourself stepping into the best version of yourself—fully engaged and open to new possibilities.

- When you are ready, gently open your eyes, knowing that this mindfulness practice has set the tone for our conversation, grounded us in the present moment and provided a space of focused attention and growth.

Let us begin our journey together.

What would you like to explore and discover today?

b) **Breath Awareness**: Coaches can incorporate breath awareness exercises during coaching conversations to bring attention to the present moment. They can guide clients to focus on their breath while noticing the inhalation and exhalation, as well as using the breath as an anchor to stay grounded. This practice helps clients enhance self-awareness during the coaching process.

Example:

- Bring your attention to your breath without trying to change it.

- Notice the natural rhythm of your breath as it flows in and out of your body.

- Pay attention to the sensation of the air entering and leaving your nostrils or the rise and fall of your chest and abdomen.

- As you continue to breathe, start counting your breaths silently in your mind. Inhale slowly to a count of four, and then exhale to the same count of four. Repeat this for a few breath cycles, focusing solely on the counting and the sensations of breathing.

As our coaching conversation unfolds, feel free to return to your breath whenever you need to centre yourself.

c) **Body Scan**: Coaches can lead clients through a body scan meditation, where clients bring awareness to different parts of their body, noticing sensations, tension and relaxation. This practice promotes somatic awareness and helps clients connect with their physical and emotional experiences. It can be particularly useful in exploring the mind-body connection and uncovering underlying emotions or patterns that impact the client's goals and development.

Example:

Body Scan for Grounding and Stress Relief:

- Find a comfortable sitting position or lie down on your back with your arms by your sides.

- Begin by taking a few deep breaths, inhale through your nose, exhale through your mouth and allow your body to relax with each breath.

- Start to bring your attention to your feet. Notice any sensation in your feet—the weight, temperature or any tension. Allow your breath to flow naturally as you focus on your feet for a few moments.

- ◆ Slowly move your attention up to your ankles and calves. Feel the sensations in these areas and any points of tension or relaxation.

- ◆ Continue to scan your body, moving up to your knees, thighs, hips, lower back, and abdomen. Take your time with each area, observing any sensations without judgement.

- ◆ Move up to your chest, upper back, shoulders, and arms. Notice how your breath flows in and out as you focus on these areas.

- ◆ Bring your attention to your neck and throat, and then up to your face. Notice any areas of tension or relaxation, and observe the sensations in your jaw, cheeks and forehead.

- ◆ Finally, focus on the top of your head and feel the sensations there.

- ◆ Take a few more deep breaths and bring your attention back to your breath as a whole.

- ◆ When you are ready, gently open your eyes if they were closed.

This body scan exercise can be used by coaches to help clients ground themselves, reduce stress and increase somatic awareness, which can be valuable for their personal and professional development.

2. **Cultivating Mindful Listening**: Coaches can encourage clients to engage in mindful listening exercises during coaching conversations. This also involves being fully present and for the coach too to be attentive to the client's words, body language and emotions without judgement or interruption. By practising mindful listening, coaches are in the service of the client fully, thus leading to valuable revelations and understandings.

Mindful Listening Exercise—Emotion Exploration

* Start by asking the client to choose an emotion or feeling that they would like to explore during the session. It could be something that they are currently experiencing or a recurring emotion that they want to understand better.

* Set aside 5–10 minutes for this exercise, depending on the complexity of the emotion that the client wants to explore.

* The client will have the opportunity to express his thoughts and feelings that are related to the chosen emotion while the coach practices mindful listening.

* During this time, the coach's role is to be fully present and attentive and give the client his undivided attention. Avoid interrupting or offering solutions—simply be there to hold space for the client's emotions.

* As the client shares, observe his body language and any shifts in his expressions. Notice if the emotion intensifies or changes throughout the exploration.

* After the client has expressed his feelings, take a few moments of silence to allow the emotions to settle and for the client to reflect on his experience.

As the coach, respond with open-ended questions that encourage deeper exploration. Ask about the client's perceptions, triggers or any insights that they gained during the exercise. Avoid imposing judgements or analyzing the emotions shared by the client. Instead, create an environment of acceptance and compassion where the client feels safe to express themselves fully.

This mindful listening exercise fosters a strong sense of trust and connection between the coach and the client.

3. **Reflective Pause:** Coaches can incorporate moments of reflective pause or silence during coaching conversations. This allows clients to process their thoughts and emotions, bringing about self-reflection.

The coach can hold the space with a mindful presence, which allows the client to evaluate their experiences and gain clarity on their goals and actions.

Reflective Pause Exercise:

First, explain the purpose of the exercise to the client—to check in with their emotions and experiences before delving into the coaching topic.

- Start the coaching session by inviting the client to take a few deep breaths and get comfortable.

- Ask the client to close their eyes if they feel comfortable doing so, or simply bring their attention inward.

- Encourage the client to notice any emotion or sensation. Are they feeling calm, anxious, excited or something else?

- Invite the client to express any emotion that comes up without judgement. It could be a single word or a short sentence, such as *calm*, *nervous about a presentation*, or *excited about a new opportunity*.

- Allow a moment of silence after the client shares their emotional check-in. Give them space to process their emotions without rushing to the next topic.

- During this reflective pause, the coach practices full presence by offering his full attention to the client.

- After a minute or two of silence, check how their emotions might relate to the coaching topic or any of their specific goals.

Use open-ended questions. For example, "How do you think your emotions might influence your approach to the upcoming presentation?"

Call attention to the fact that the reflective pause is a valuable moment in making more intentional decisions and actions.

This reflective pause exercise allows the client to begin the coaching session with self-awareness and mindfulness, which leads to more impactful coaching conversations.

4. **Walking Meditation**: Coaches can motivate their clients to actively try out this practice, which involves walking slowly and mindfully, as well as paying attention to each step, the sensations in the body and the surroundings. It combines movement with mindfulness and offers a refreshing and grounding practice for those who find sitting meditation challenging. The coach can even try to have a full-fledged coaching session that is conducted as a 'walk in nature'.

Nature Connection Walk

Duration: 30–60 minutes

Location: Find a quiet and natural outdoor setting, such as a park, forest trail or beach.

Instructions for the Client:

- Begin by taking a few deep breaths to centre yourself and clear your mind. Set the intention to be fully present and open to the experience.

- As you start walking, focus your attention on the sensations of each step. Feel the ground beneath your feet, the shifting weight from one foot to the other and the gentle rhythm of your walking.

- Engage your senses in the experience. Notice the sights, sounds and smells around you. Observe the colours of the leaves, the rustling of the trees, the chirping of birds or the sound of waves crashing on the shore.

- Allow yourself to slow down and connect with nature. Pause at times to touch the bark of a tree or feel the texture of a flower.

- As you walk, reflect on any challenges, questions or goals that you want to explore during the coaching session. Be open to any insights or inspirations that arise during the walk.

- When you feel ready to start the session, find a peaceful spot to sit down. Take a few moments to meditate on the experience and its connection to your coaching goals.

- Once done, continue your walk at a leisurely pace, and remain attentive to your surroundings and your thoughts.

- When you are ready to conclude the walk, take a moment to express gratitude for the time spent in nature and the insights gained.

Instructions for the Coach:

- As the coach, walk alongside the client, yet let them have a reflective space. Be with the client as they immerse themselves in the natural environment.

- During the walk, allow moments of silence for introspection to happen. Pose open-ended questions if needed to deepen the client's experience.

- Be attentive to any non-verbal cues or shifts in the client's energy during the walk. Use these as prompts for further inquiry when appropriate.

- Once the client is seated and ready for deeper discussion, transition smoothly into the coaching session, and build upon what came up for the client during the walk.

By combining the healing power of nature with the practice of mindful walking, this coaching exercise creates a unique and powerful experience for clients.

5. **Guided Visualization**: Guided visualization is a technique used in mindful meditation where individuals are guided through a specific scenario or mental imagery to evoke a desired experience or outcome. It involves using the power of imagination to create a vivid and sensory-rich mental picture.

During guided visualization, a coach or meditation facilitator provides verbal instructions to help individuals imagine themselves in a particular situation, such as a peaceful natural setting or a future success scenario. They may ask individuals to even visualize specific details, sensations and emotions associated with the scene.

The purpose is to facilitate relaxation, focus and optimistic thoughts. It can be used to reduce stress, increase self-confidence, improve performance or achieve a sense of inner peace.

Guided visualization can be conducted through in-person sessions, audio recordings or guided meditation apps. It is a powerful tool for channelling the mind's potential and bringing about helpful changes in thoughts, emotions and behaviour.

Here is an example of a guided visualization for mindfulness meditation:

Guided Visualization: The Inner Sanctuary

Duration: 5–10 minutes

- Find a quiet corner in your office or step outside to a nearby park during a break.

- Take a moment to sit comfortably with your feet on the ground and your hands resting on your lap.

- Take a few deep breaths to relax.

- Imagine yourself in the heart of a bustling city, surrounded by tall buildings and busy streets. Despite the chaos around you, you notice a hidden oasis nearby.

- See yourself in your mind's eye standing at the entrance of a beautiful garden.

- Picture the gate and notice the details—the colour, texture, and design.

- As you walk through the gate, you enter the serene and peaceful garden filled with vibrant flowers, tall trees and a gently blowing breeze.

- Take a moment to scan the garden and note the sights, sounds and scents around you.

- Feel the soft grass beneath your feet and the warm sunlight on your skin.

- In the centre of the garden, you see a small pathway leading to a hidden sanctuary. Follow the path and feel a sense of anticipation and curiosity.

- As you arrive at the sanctuary, you see a serene and inviting space. It could be a cosy cabin, a quiet temple or any place that feels safe and comforting to you.

- Step inside the sanctuary and take a moment to look around. Catch sight of the details of the space and objects that bring you a sense of quietude.

- Find a comfortable spot to sit or lie down. Take a deep breath and allow yourself to fully relax.

- Now, bring your attention to your breath. Notice the sensation of each inhale and exhale. Allow a sense of release and let go of any tension or worries.

- As you continue to breathe, visualize a soft, warm light filling the sanctuary. This light represents love, compassion, and inner peace.

- Feel the warmth of this light encompassing you and bringing you a sense of comfort and security.

- As you bask in this loving light, repeat a positive affirmation silently to yourself. It could be a simple phrase like, "I am calm and centred," or any affirmation that resonates with you.

- Stay in this inner sanctuary for a few more moments, soaking in the love and peace that surrounds you.

- When you are ready, take a deep breath and slowly open your eyes.

Carry this calm and quiet from the urban oasis with you as you resume your busy day, knowing that you have this inner sanctuary to return to whenever you need a moment of peace.

This guided imagery exercise aids individuals in developing mindfulness by directing their focus to the current moment, bringing in a sense of serenity and tranquillity.

6. **Integration into Action Plans**: Mindfulness meditation practices can be commingled into clients' action plans/daily routines as a way to boost self-awareness. This practice emerges as a powerful ally in coaching—a life-changing tool.

Picture this—clients engaging in daily routines while drawing in from the magic of mindfulness exercises, to manage stress and stay laser-focused on their goals.

The best is that each coach affords an exclusive and tailored experience.

Envision clients conquering overwhelm, eliciting their inner wisdom and reaching new heights. This is not a one-size-fits-all approach. It is a personalized approach, carefully curated to suit each client's hopes and dreams, as each client discovers the art of mindful living with newfound grace and purpose.

It is important to note that the specific use of mindfulness and meditation practices will vary based on the coach's training, client needs and coaching approach. Coaches should always adapt these practices to suit the individual client's comfort level and goals, which ensures a caring and effective coaching experience.

A Zen Story:

A man was travelling across a field when he encountered a tiger. He began to run, and the tiger chased after him. Coming to a precipice, he slipped and was able to catch hold of the root of a wild strawberry bush, hanging in the air. The tiger sniffed at him from above. Trembling, the man looked down only to find that another tiger was waiting to eat him. He thought the bush could sustain him for a while until he saw two mice gnawing away the vine.

A tiger above, a tiger below.

The man saw a ripe strawberry near him. Grabbing the vine with one hand, he plucked the strawberry with the other and ate it. "How sweet and delicious, he mused."

Buddhism teaches us the essence of living in the present, fully alive in the here and now.

Conclusion:

Within this chapter, we've grasped the potent fusion of mindfulness meditation and coaching. As a sturdy instrument, mindfulness meditation equips coaches to strengthen interpersonal bonds, lend unwavering ears, and guide with authenticity. Through self-awareness, presence, and compassion, coaches establish room for radical development. This chapter attests to the transcendence of mindfulness meditation, beyond technique, into the bedrock of coaching, benefitting both coach and client.

Resolutely train yourself to attain peace.

– Buddha

Chapter 9

Leadership Excellence

A Buddhist Parable That Illustrates the Role of Wisdom:

Once, there was a young monk who was deeply committed to his meditation practice. However, despite his sincere efforts, he felt frustrated with his lack of progress and the barriers he faced. Feeling disheartened, he approached his teacher and sought guidance.

The wise teacher, seeing his predicament, took him to a nearby musical instrument—a stringed lute. The teacher asked, "What happens when the lute string is too tight?"

He replied, "It produces a harsh and unpleasant sound."

The teacher then asked, "And what happens when the lute string is too loose?"

He replied, "It produces a weak and ineffective sound."

The teacher gently smiled and said, "Just like the lute string, your meditation practice requires balance and wisdom. Too much effort can lead to tension and annoyance, while too little effort can result in stagnation. Find the right balance—the Middle Way, between striving and letting go. Be sagacious when to apply effort and when to relax, letting the practice unfold naturally."

The parable features the role of wisdom in Buddhism. Wisdom enables us to discern the importance of balance, thus understanding that excessive striving or complacency can hinder progress. With newfound perceptiveness, individuals can realign their actions and methods to harmonise with the present moment and their specific situations.

In Chapter 9, the role of wisdom comes to the forefront in Buddhism and coaching. We understand how wisdom can act as a compass for coaches in presenting thought-provoking inquiries, invaluable outlooks, and in clients' self-evolution.

In Buddhism, wisdom plays a principal role and is one of the two key components of the *Noble Eightfold Path*, along with ethical conduct (*sila*) and meditation (*samadhi*).

Wisdom is represented by two interconnected aspects—right understanding (*samma ditthi*) and right thought (*samma sankappa*).

Right understanding involves seeing and perceiving reality as it truly is—free from delusions and misconceptions.

Right thought refers to harbouring wholesome and beneficial thoughts that are free from attachment, ill-will, and harmful intentions. It involves developing non-sabotaging attitudes towards oneself and others. Right thought directs the mind towards qualities that reflect magnanimity and supports the practice of ethical conduct.

Wisdom in Buddhism is not merely an unattainable perfection or intellectual knowledge but a transformative understanding that evolves over time. It is acquired through personal experience, meditation, and guidance from wise teachers.

Right Understanding

In the context of workplace dynamics, the parallel to the right understanding in Buddhism can be seen in the following ways:

1. **Seeing and perceiving reality as it truly is:** In the workplace, the right understanding involves recognizing the current state of affairs without distortion or bias.

   It is important to spend a little time here to understand BIAS.

   Bias can be defined as *a predisposition or preference for a particular person, group or perspective.* They are usually not based on fact or reason but rather, a combination of factors, such as age, gender, race, culture, personal experience and more. Because they are not fact-based, biases can often result in unfair treatment towards a person or group of people. Gordon Allport, the author of *The Nature of Prejudice*, explains that bias is a result of our very human tendency to classify people into categories in order to quickly process information and make sense of the world around us (Allport, 1954). [56]

Source of bias:

a) **Cultural and Societal Norms**: Cultural expectations and social norms can shape our beliefs and attitudes against marginalized groups in areas, such as employment, education, and healthcare, which leads to discrimination and prejudice.

b) **Personal Experiences**: Negative encounters with individuals from specific groups can influence our perceptions and behaviours towards others in the same group.

c) **Cognitive Processes**: Cognitive biases, such as confirmation bias or stereotypes, can cause us to overlook contradictory information and rely on mental shortcuts leading to error-prone judgement and decision-making.

We must know that bias is a pervasive influence that impacts our thoughts, decisions and interactions in subtle yet powerful ways. Understanding the different types of bias is crucial in our endeavour towards building a more just and inclusive world rooted in compassion.

Here are some examples of these biases and their damaging effects:

- **Implicit Bias**: Implicit biases are unconscious attitudes and stereotypes that shape our perceptions and judgements about others, often without our awareness. They can perpetuate harmful generalisations and contribute to unfair treatment and discrimination.

  Imagine a hiring manager reviewing job applications. Despite their best intentions, they unconsciously favour candidates from their race or gender, leading to unintentional discrimination and overlooking qualified candidates from diverse backgrounds.

- **Confirmation Bias**: Confirmation bias is our tendency to seek out information that confirms our pre-existing beliefs while ignoring or dismissing conflicting evidence. It reinforces narrow perspectives and hinders our ability to consider alternative viewpoints.

  A person reads an article that supports their political views and shares it on social media without fact-checking. They ignore other well-researched articles with opposing stances, wrongly corroborating their existing beliefs and polarizing their social circle.

- **Anchoring Bias**: Anchoring bias occurs when we rely too heavily on the first piece of information we receive when making decisions. It limits our exploration of other options and can lead to flawed judgements.

  A consumer sees a product with a high price tag in a store and assumes it must be of superior quality. They fail to check out other choices at different price points, potentially missing out on more affordable products that are equally good.

- **Availability Bias**: The availability bias influences our judgement based on information that is readily available in our memory. We give more weight to recent or vivid examples, even if they may not represent the overall reality. This bias can lead to inaccurate assessments and misjudgements.

  After seeing a few news reports about shark attacks, a person becomes overly fearful of swimming in the ocean, even though the probability of a shark attack is quite low. They let vivid and emotional media coverage dictate their perception of risk.

- **Halo Bias**: Halo bias refers to our tendency to form an overall positive impression of a person based on one prominent positive characteristic or attribute. It can result in overlooking other aspects and potential shortcomings, leading to biased assessments and evaluations.

A manager commends an employee for his exceptional public speaking skills, leading him to also assume that the employee is equally proficient in other areas, such as problem-solving or teamwork, without sufficient evidence.

- **Ingroup Bias:** Ingroup bias is the tendency to favour individuals who belong to the same group or share similar characteristics or beliefs as ourselves. It can lead to favouritism, exclusion of outgroup members and perpetuate social divisions.

During a group project, team members tend to allocate more responsibilities to their friends or colleagues they are familiar with, overlooking the valuable contributions of outsiders or individuals from different departments.

- **Cultural Bias**: Cultural bias involves prioritizing certain cultural norms, values, or behaviours over others. It can marginalize individuals from different cultural backgrounds and hinder cross-cultural understanding and collaboration.

A company implements a standardized dress code that aligns with the dominant culture, which may inadvertently exclude employees who wear cultural or religious attire that is different from the norm.

- **Systemic Bias**: Systemic bias refers to biases embedded within societal structures, institutions, and policies. They perpetuate inequalities and discrimination on a systemic level, impacting marginalized groups. Addressing systemic biases requires collective effort and structural change.

A country's educational system disproportionately funds schools in affluent neighbourhoods while neglecting underprivileged communities. As a result, students from marginalized areas have limited access to quality education and resources, perpetuating societal disparities.

These biases have detrimental impacts, adversely influencing our decision-making, relationships and overall societal dynamics. They can lead to unintended consequences as missed opportunities and reinforce existing power imbalances. Being aware of these biases can help individuals and organizations make more informed and equitable choices. It is our shared responsibility to dismantle biases and create a world that compassionately views the richness of our differences.

Bias in the Workplace

Bias in the workplace can manifest in various forms, such as hiring biases, promotion biases or unfair treatment. In the workplace, right understanding involves recognizing that diversity and inclusion are essential for innovation and success. Instead of holding onto the belief that certain groups or individuals are inherently better or worse, a person with right understanding acknowledges the uniqueness and varied talents each individual brings to the table ultimately leading to more informed decisions and creative problem-solving. This promotes a workplace culture that values and respects differences where everyone can thrive.

In the context of Buddhist wisdom, beating bias requires a high level of awareness and compassion.

The teachings of Buddhism emphasize the recognition of interconnectedness and the inherent worth and dignity of all beings. It is highly relevant in today's DEI (diversity, equity, and inclusion) efforts. The latter becomes a fertile ground for according respect and appreciation to others leading to more inclusive and harmonious societies.

Let's look at some DEI trends and statistics and their impact:

A) **Employee Engagement**: Diverse and inclusive workplaces have been linked to higher levels of employee engagement. A study by Deloitte found that organizations with inclusive cultures are six times more likely to be innovative and agile.[57]

B) **Customer Satisfaction and Financial Performance**: Companies that prioritize DEI often outperform their competitors. The Harvard Business Review reported that organizations with above-average diversity on their executive teams had higher innovation revenue and were more likely to capture new markets.[58]

C) **Talent Acquisition and Retention**: Inclusive companies are more attractive to job seekers, particularly younger generations. According to a survey by Glassdoor[1] 67% of job seekers consider diversity an important factor when evaluating potential employers.[59]

Finally, recognizing bias and understanding its impact is crucial for endorsing inclusivity and realising a more equitable society.

2. **Free from delusions and misconceptions**: Right understanding requires relinquishing falsely held pre-determined notions as well as misleading and misinformed beliefs that may hinder progress. It involves rising above suppositions or speculations and being open to new information.

Delusions are false or distorted beliefs that individuals hold, often influenced by the above-stated biases, stereotypes or personal judgements.

Misconceptions are misunderstandings or incorrect interpretations of information or situations.

Delusion

Example 1. Believing that one's cultural background is superior to others, leading to biases and discrimination.

---

1   *The statistics here are for a general understanding of DEI trends and one must validate them with up-to-date research and industry-specific data for a more comprehensive analysis.*

Remedy: Engaging in cultural sensitivity training and cross-cultural exchanges, promoting interfaith dialogue, encouraging religious tolerance and actively seeking to understand and appreciate diverse cultures.

Example 2. Thinking that individuals with disabilities are incapable of contributing to the workforce.

Remedy: Celebrating inclusivity and accessibility, providing reasonable accommodations and valuing the prolific skillsets and competencies of people with disabilities.

Misconception

Example 1: Assuming that introverted individuals lack leadership skills and overlooking their unique strengths and contributions.

Remedy: Acknowledging multifarious personality traits, providing platforms for different communication styles and investing in building inclusive environments that stand by collaboration.

Example 2: Believing that mental health struggles are a sign of weakness, which leads to stigmatization and hindering support-seeking behaviours.

Remedy: Promoting mental health awareness, educating about the importance of well-being and scaffolding a culture of empathy and support.

Scenario: A modern workplace

A team leader who realizes that their preferred management style may not be effective for all team members remains open to different approaches, seeks feedback and adjusts his methods accordingly.

This illustrates how right understanding in the workplace involves a clear and unbiased perception of reality, and furthers a more productive and harmonious work environment.

One popular model that aligns with the example provided is the widely acclaimed and read, the Situational Leadership® Model developed by Paul

Hersey and Kenneth Blanchard. This model highlights the importance of adapting leadership style based on the readiness or development level of team members. Other models, such as the Transformational Leadership Model or the Servant Leadership Model also underscore adaptability and responsiveness in leadership approaches.

After a year of dedicated exploration, I have developed a ground-breaking model that revolutionizes the approach to "adaptive leadership". This innovative framework is derived from the timeless teachings of Buddhist wisdom and ancient traditions, which propels leaders towards the pinnacle of leadership brilliance.

Meta-leadership: Channelling Collective Intelligence for Adaptive Excellence

Meta-leadership is an approach that revolutionizes the concept of adaptive leadership by tapping into the collective intelligence and expertise of a diverse network and affords the convergence of disciplines to address complex challenges.

1. Holistic Illumination: Essence is—Networked Thinking

Leaders embody the role of *praevidere*—the visionary seeker who perceives the interconnectedness of diverse systems and stakeholders. They engage in *nexus cognition*—a heightened state of awareness that unveils hidden patterns and emerging trends. By embracing this ancient wisdom, leaders tap into the power of *vasutara*—the universal web of interconnectedness to synthesize knowledge and make informed decisions.

They embrace a holistic view, leveraging the knowledge and expertise of diverse individuals and groups.

2. Harmonious Convergence: Essence is—Collaborative Intelligence

Leaders foster a culture of *sahaja sambandha*—natural interconnectedness, where collaboration, dialogue and empathy flourish. They become *sangathakarta*, the orchestrators of collective intelligence, which create spaces for *sambhodhana*—respectful and inclusive conversations. Through *samanvaya sutra*—the thread of harmony, leaders facilitate the convergence of diverse perspectives and harness the wisdom of the collective to co-create innovative solutions.

Leaders foster an inclusive and participatory culture.

3. Agile Elevation: Essence Is—Adaptive Learning

Leaders embrace *anuvriddhi shiksha*, the continuous growth mindset and push their teams to become *swayamvruddha*—self-evolving individuals. They bring in a culture of *nirantara abhyasa*—constant experimentation and learning from experiences. By invoking the spirit of *kshamata vikas*—capacity development, leaders empower their teams to adapt, innovate, and thrive amidst uncertainty, and propel the organization towards adaptive excellence.

Leaders further a culture of continuous learning and experimentation.

With *Meta-leadership*, organizations transcend traditional leadership paradigms and harness the power of collective intelligence to spark great transformations.

Right Thought

Moving ahead, in the modern context, the parallel to *right thought* in Buddhism can be understood by considering the following examples and related challenges:

1. **Shifting from Negative to Positive Mindset**: One of the common human traits we toil with is dealing with setbacks or difficult situations that can lead to negative thinking. For example, when faced with a project failure, a person with right thought would strive to realign and move from dwelling on the failure to treasuring the lessons learned and grabbing favourable prospects in the future. This helps to sustain motivation, resilience and a positive outlook amidst challenges.

2. **Balancing Ambition and Contentment**: In a competitive work environment, individuals may feel pressured to constantly strive for more success and recognition. Right thought encourages finding a balance between ambition and contentment, where individuals can pursue their goals and aspirations while appreciating their present accomplishments and finding repose in the journey.

3. **Embracing Change and Uncertainty**: In today's world, we are charging ahead at a break-neck speed and therefore adapting to change is crucial rather than resisting it out of fear or clinging to the familiar. This stance enables individuals to be more in tune with times and novel in tackling new-age dilemmas and questions.

4. **Matching Individual and Collective Goals**: In increasingly fluid work environments, conflicts may arise when individual goals clash with the larger objectives of the team or organization. Right thought propels individuals to consider the greater good and find solutions that benefit both individual and mutual aspirations.

5. **Developing Compassion in a Multicultural Workforce**: As already discussed in detail, with right thought as a foundation for compassion, we can build cohesive teams that serve all.

Let's consider a new strategy to actionize the above idea!

Empathy Bridge

Let us look at *Empathy Bridge* in action:

In a high-pressure project, the marketing team faces a critical decision that could impact the success of their campaign. Emma, a team member, strongly advocates for a bold and innovative approach while David, another teammate, insists on a more conservative and data-driven strategy. Tensions rise as their differing opinions clash, which threatens to derail the project.

Recognizing the need for effective collaboration, James, the team leader, applies the Empathy Bridge approach. He organizes a dedicated meeting where Emma and David can find room and sense psychological safety to verbalize their concerns and perspectives openly. James actively listens to their arguments, handholding them objectively to examine their underlying motivations and values.

Through this process, Emma reveals her passion for creativity and taking risks to achieve breakthrough results. David, on the other hand, shares his commitment to data-driven decision-making and ensuring a solid return on investment. James facilitates a constructive dialogue, which calls for empathy and consideration.

As they grasp the depth of each other's viewpoints, Emma and David start to appreciate the validity of their respective arguments. They discover common ground by blending innovation with a measured approach that respects data and mitigates risks. With the newfound understanding, they join forces on a revised campaign strategy that includes both their perspectives and results in a powerful and well-balanced marketing campaign.

The Empathy Bridge approach, facilitated by James, not only resolves the conflict but also strengthens the team's bond. Emma and David realize that their divergent opinions can be complementary and lead to better outcomes when approached with tolerance and love. The success of the campaign establishes the credibility of the Empathy Bridge approach.

Let's look into the Empathy Bridge in action through a tangible scenario:

Imagine you're a project manager facing a testing situation that could significantly impact the project's outcome. To use the Empathy Bridge approach, consider these steps:

a) **Recognize the Conflict**: Acknowledge the differing opinions and potential conflicts within your team. Understand that these differences can lead to creative solutions if managed effectively.

b) Provide a Safe Space: Organize a dedicated meeting where team members can openly express their viewpoints without fear of judgement. Set a respectful and inclusive tone for the discussion.

c) Active Listening: As the facilitator, actively listen to each person's perspective. Be genuinely interested to know more about their ideas, motivations, and concerns. Allow them to share their thoughts without interruption.

d) Probe for Values: Ask probing questions that look into the values and motivations behind each viewpoint. Understand what drives their suggestions and why they believe their approach is the best.

e) Identify Common Ground: During the dialogue, look for common threads or shared goals between the opposing viewpoints. Highlight areas of agreement to build a foundation for compromise.

f) Champion Empathy: Urge team members to put themselves in each other's shoes. This helps them understand the emotions and reasons behind their colleagues' opinions.

g) Blend Perspectives: Steer the conversation towards finding a solution that combines the best aspects of both viewpoints. Call for brainstorming and creative problem-solving to attain a well-rounded approach.

h) Prioritise Collaboration: Restate that the goal is a collective success. Point out how combining different strengths and perspectives can lead to novel and comprehensive solutions.

i) Test and Refine: Implement the blended approach in a controlled setting or pilot project. Monitor its effectiveness and be open to refining it based on real-world results.

j) Celebrate Success: Once you've successfully navigated the conflict and achieved positive outcomes, celebrate the team's achievement. Recognize the importance of understanding and collaboration in achieving the project's goals.

6. **Practising Mindfulness Amidst Distractions**: The modern work environment is often filled with distractions, such as multitasking, constant notifications and information overload. Right thought emphasizes mindfulness, which involves being fully present and aware in the moment. It means consciously focusing on one task at a time, actively listening to others during meetings and managing distractions to maintain clarity and productivity. For example, an employee takes a mindful pause before responding to a challenging email and allows himself to regain focus and respond with clarity and intention instead of reacting impulsively.

7. **Letting Go of Ego and Comparison**: In today's cut-throat world, the ego-driven desire for recognition and comparison with others can mar personal growth and create a stressful environment. Right thought enables individuals to let go of ego-driven thoughts and concentrate on their contributions and forward movement, thus cherishing their inimitable strengths and qualities.

For example, instead of being drawn into unhelpful comparisons of their progress with others, a professional chooses to bring their attention to the milestones they wish to achieve while celebrating the accomplishments of their colleagues.

By relating the concept of right thought in Buddhism to these modern workplace challenges, individuals can understand its practical application. By applying its principles, we can hope for a world full of solidarity marked by compassion towards self and others.

After discussing how Buddhist wisdom applies to the corporate world, we see its relevance in coaching leaders and any individual for that matter. The principles of right understanding and right thought, initially explored in the context of the corporate world, seamlessly extend to the realm of coaching. This continuity underscores the adaptability and universality of these principles, showcasing their application in diverse contexts, including supporting clients through Buddhist compassion coaching.

Cultivating Right Understanding: Coaches can use their understanding of reality as it truly is to challenge the status quo with thought-provoking questions that examine clients' limiting beliefs and open up new doors.

For example, a coach may ask, "What assumptions are you making about this situation, and how might they be limiting your perspective?"

Nurturing Right Thought: Coaches can help clients develop wholesome and beneficial thoughts. They can inspire clients to let go of attachments, resentments and harmful intentions.

For instance, a coach may say, "Consider viewing this setback as a chance for further growth rather than as a roadblock. How might this shift in perspective look for you?"

Supporting in Knowing Self: Coaches can facilitate mindfulness practices that promote self-reflection and help clients access their inner wisdom.

For example, a coach may invite a client to take a few moments of silence and ask, "What insights arise when you tune into your inner wisdom and let go of external distractions?"

By incorporating Buddhist principles of right understanding and right thought into their coaching approach, coaches can create wonders.

Conclusion:

This chapter thoroughly examined the central role of wisdom within the realm of compassionate coaching and leadership. It brought to the forefront the potential for long-lasting change that results from bringing together Buddhist wisdom with coaching practices, honing attributes like empathy, collaboration, and substantive influence. The insights gleaned from this work serve as a poignant reminder that leadership surpasses mere authority—it involves promoting self-awareness, compassion, and interconnectedness. The journey through Leadership Excellence, yields a narrative that transcends the ordinary and leaves a lasting mark of purpose and significance.

Irrigators channel waters; fletchers straighten arrows; carpenters bend wood; the wise master themselves.

– Buddha

Balancing Buddhism, Compassion and Coaching

In Chapter 10, we see the practical application of the fusion of Buddhism, compassion, and coaching, which forms a dynamic framework that creates a holistic approach to personal and professional development. We analyse real-life examples, case studies and exercises to apply the concepts that are discussed.

Buddhist Social Work: A Case Study of the Samrong General Hospital, Bangkok.

Overview of the Samrong General Hospital

The hospital was established in 1981 by a couple of medical doctors who desired to have a place to save the lives of patients and injured people in the Samut Prakan province. Before that, it was very difficult to access remote hospitals in Bangkok and many patients would die before being able to receive medical treatment. When they opened the private clinic, there were only two hospitals available but now, there are 26 private hospitals nearby. Thus, it is highly competitive for the healthcare business in that area but the 250-bed Samrong General Hospital remains one of the leading medical institutions in the Samut Prakan province because of its policies, management principles, and—as it is claimed—Buddhist-based organizational practices.

Founders Dr Sutep and Dr Prapa Wongphaet graduated from German universities and had a clear vision which stated "This hospital will save patients' lives and help them get better. We do not want to make any business or look only for profits from patients' lives."

Consequently, they have never asked any patient, "Do you have money?"

Or they have never asked them to make a deposit in advance before helping them (Wongphaet, 2011; Wongsutal, 2011).[60]

The first thing for all employees to do for patients is to help and save their lives.

The research is based on Buddhist ethical principles and focuses on the implementation of these principles. The hospital's founders aimed to create an ethical and compassionate environment rather than prioritizing specific tasks or benefits.

The study included interviews and a focus group to explore the hospital's Buddhist social work scheme.

The hospital promotes Buddhist concepts among staff members and puts emphasis on the principles of the *five precepts*, the basis of success (*Iddhipada* 4), the sublime states of mind (*Brahmavihāra* 4), and *meditation*. These principles are believed to contribute to ethical behaviour and improved job performance.

The hospital's policies revolve around doing good and righteous actions, including transparency in accounting and financial systems. They refuse to perform morally questionable procedures. The hospital aims to be a safe shelter and prioritizes patient care and well-being over revenue.

The organizational culture at the hospital is shaped by various projects and activities based on Buddhist principles. These include inexpensive lunch programmes, subsidized rental apartments, discounted shoes, scholarship opportunities and monthly activities for making merits and practising *Dhamma*. [Dhamma is the core teachings of Buddhism, guiding us towards understanding, compassion, and personal growth.] The hospital also engages in external activities, such as health education, free physical check-ups, anti-drug programmes, and community support through the Samrong Ruamjai Foundation.

The founders and top management create a paternalistic environment and treat employees like family members. The hospital also makes sure to train staff in providing compassionate care, particularly in the ICU, and shows movies, such as *Departures* to inspire moral values and empathy.

Overall, the Samrong General Hospital interlaces Buddhist principles into its organizational structure and practices, underscoring honourable behaviour, compassionate care and spiritual development among its staff members.[61]

One of the important Buddhist principles incorporated by Samrong General Hospital is the concept of the *sublime states of mind*, also known as *Brahmavihāra* 4. This virtue encompasses four qualities:

1. *Mettā:* It refers to loving-kindness, friendliness, and goodwill. It involves having a compassionate and caring attitude towards all beings and wishing them happiness and well-being.

2. *Karuṇā:* It represents compassion, which entails a deep empathy for the suffering of others. It involves actively seeking ways to alleviate their suffering and provide support and assistance.

3. *Muditā:* It signifies sympathetic joy or altruistic joy. It means rejoicing in the happiness and success of others without any trace of envy or jealousy. It involves genuinely celebrating the well-being and achievements of others.

4. *Upekkhā:* It conveys the concept of equanimity, poise, and neutrality. It involves developing a balanced and non-reactive mindset, being able to maintain composure in both favourable and unfavourable circumstances and treating all beings impartially.

These four qualities of *Brahmavihāra* 4 are considered to be the *Dhamma* of *Brahma*, thus representing the *Dhamma* principle for human beings. By cultivating these sublime states of mind, individuals can lead wholesome and honest lives which further the well-being of the self and all.

The Buddhist principle of the sublime states of mind falls in line closely with the values and goals of coaching.

The concept of *Mettā* in Buddhism, stressing loving-kindness and goodwill, finds resonance in coaching relationships. Coaches hold a safe and non-judgemental space for clients, which furthers their growth and self-acceptance through unconditional positive regard.

In Buddhism, compassion, represented by *Karuṇā*, lies at the heart of a true desire for easing the suffering of others. Similarly, coaching is rooted in a compassionate approach, as coaches strive to understand and 'feel with' their clients' life's ups and downs and support them in seeing ways to advance.

Muditā, the Buddhist principle of sympathetic joy, is parallel to coaching's focus on celebrating clients' successes and achievements. With a sense of genuine joy and encouragement, coaches acknowledge clients' accomplishments and find inspiration in their progress.

Furthermore, the Buddhist principle of *Upekkhā*, embodying equanimity and neutrality can be valuable in coaching. Coaches strive to maintain a balanced perspective, remaining non-reactive to their clients' challenges and helping them sail through trying times with calmness and clarity.

To illustrate these concepts, here are some examples:

a) Imagine a coach working with a business executive who is striving to improve his leadership skills. The coach may integrate the principles of *mettā* (loving-kindness) and *karuṇā* (compassion) by encouraging the executive to genuinely listen to his team members' concerns and challenges. By expressing kindness and dealing with grace, the executive can build trust and healthier team dynamics, thus leading to increased employee morale and productivity.

b) In another scenario, a coach working with a young athlete may incorporate *muditā* (sympathetic joy) by helping the athlete celebrate the achievements and successes of their teammates. By partaking in the team's triumphs with a shared sense of joy, the athlete can develop a stronger sense of camaraderie and motivation, which contributes to improved team dynamics and performance.

c) Lastly, a coach working with an individual going through a difficult life transition may focus on *upekkhā* (equanimity). By guiding the client to approach tribulations with a sense of calm and acceptance, the coach can help them steer through the uncertainties and changes with greater fortitude.

Here are some exercises that can help you integrate these principles:

i. **Compassion Circles**: In this approach, participants can join group activities such as meditation, reflective sharing, and compassionate listening. As a coach, you can facilitate these circles for individuals [in teams] to deepen their connection with themselves and others through the lens of Buddhism.

ii. **Values-based Coaching**: Incorporate Buddhist principles and values into your coaching practice. Help your clients identify their core values. Check how it would be to explore concepts such as compassion, mindfulness and non-attachment as driving principles for decision-making and personal growth.

iii. **Mindful Goal Setting**: This approach takes into cognisance the importance of compassionate action so clients can consider the welfare of all beings in their pursuit of goals instead of being solely fixated on external achievements. Incorporate mindfulness practices into the goal-setting process to help clients become aware of their intentions, motivations and the impact of their conduct on themselves and others.

Remember, it is important to tailor these approaches to suit the needs and value systems of your clients. Integrating Buddhism, compassion and coaching requires sensitivity and respect for individual beliefs and preferences.

New research and evidence support the effectiveness of these approaches. Here are some reputable agencies and organizations that have conducted studies in these areas:

1. **Mindful Presence:**

Mindfulness-based Stress Reduction (MBSR): Developed by Jon Kabat-Zinn, MBSR has been extensively researched and studied for its benefits in stress reduction and bettering overall well-being. The Centre for Mindfulness in Medicine, Health Care and Society at the University of Massachusetts Medical School is a prominent institution that conducts research on MBSR.[62]

- A study conducted by Tang et al. (2019) examined the effects of mindfulness-based interventions (MBIs) on well-being and psychological distress. The results showed that participants who received MBIs reported notable improvements.[63]

- A meta-analysis by Khoury et al. (2013) reviewed 209 studies on mindfulness-based interventions and found that they were effective in reducing anxiety, depression and stress and increasing the quality of life.[64]

2. **Compassion Circles:**

Centre for Compassion and Altruism Research and Education (CCARE): Based at Stanford University, CCARE conducts research on compassion, empathy and altruism. They explore the effects of compassion training programmes and practices on individuals' holistic health and interpersonal relationships.[65]

- A study conducted by Klimecki et al. (2014) investigated the impact of compassion training on neural responses to suffering. The findings revealed that individuals who underwent compassion training showed increased activation in brain regions associated with empathy and positive emotions when witnessing others in distress.[66]

- A systematic review by Kirby et al. (2017) examined the effects of compassion-focused interventions on mental health outcomes. The review indicated that compassion interventions were associated with lower symptoms of depression, anxiety and stress, as well as increased self-compassion and good health.[67]

3. **Values-based Coaching:**

The Institute of Coaching: Affiliated with McLean Hospital, a Harvard Medical School affiliate, the Institute of Coaching promotes evidence-based coaching practices. They provide resources, research and access to studies related to coaching and personal development.

*   A study by Grant and Schwartz (2011) explored the effectiveness of values-based coaching in enhancing goal attainment and well-being. The results indicated that participants who received values-based coaching experienced greater goal progress, improved well-being and increased job satisfaction compared to those who received traditional coaching.[68]

*   A meta-analysis by Richardson (2008) examined the impact of values-based interventions on various outcomes. The findings suggested that values-based interventions were effective in promoting goal attainment, motivation, and well-being.[69]

4. **Mindful Goal Setting:**

Positive Psychology: Positive psychology research explores the connection between goal setting, well-being, and flourishing. The Positive Psychology Centre at the University of Pennsylvania, led by Martin Seligman, conducts research in this field.

*   A study by Latham and Locke (2007) examined the relationship between goal setting and performance. The research demonstrated that setting specific and challenging goals led to higher levels of performance compared to vague or no goals.[70]

*   A meta-analysis by Harkin et al. (2016) investigated the effects of goal setting on well-being. The results showed that setting goals, which were personally meaningful and aligned with one's values and interests positively impacted well-being.[71]

These studies and findings provide evidence for the effectiveness of mindfulness, compassion, values-based approaches and goal setting in various contexts. While the direct integration of Buddhism may not always be studied explicitly, these agencies and organizations provide meaningful perspectives and evidence in related fields that can inform and support the integration of Buddhism, compassion and coaching and how these related concepts and practices when incorporated into coaching approaches promote *optimal living* and *self-growth*.

Real-life Examples:

- Companies, such as Google, Apple, and Intel have introduced mindfulness programmes and meditation rooms in their workplaces to support employee well-being and enhance productivity.

- The Compassion Cultivation Training (CCT) programme, developed by researchers at Stanford University, offers a structured curriculum to cultivate compassion and empathy. CCT has been implemented in various settings, including healthcare, education, and community organizations.[72]

- The Centre for Values-driven Leadership at Benedictine University offers a values-based coaching programme that combines coaching principles with attention to personal values and ethics. This approach helps individuals align their actions with their core values and brings in a sense of purpose and fulfilment.[73]

- The Barrett Values Centre provides tools and resources for coaches and organizations to assess and align values within the workplace. Their cultural transformation tools help identify value gaps and guide the development of a values-driven organizational culture.[74]

- The University of California, Berkeley's Greater Good Science Centre conducts research and offers resources on the application of mindfulness and compassion in various domains, including coaching. They investigate the benefits of incorporating Buddhist principles in coaching interventions to realise wellness and wholeness.[75]

The practices and approaches mentioned have been implemented and applied in various contexts, with anecdotal evidence and qualitative feedback supporting their effectiveness.

Conclusion:

Chapter 10 revealed a practical journey, illustrating the concrete integration of Buddhism, compassion, and coaching principles. Through real-life examples and case studies, we explored the application of these concepts in coaching scenarios. We witnessed the effect of this fusion on individuals' personal and professional development, as well as on the dynamics of coaching relationships. This chapter acted as a clear roadmap for coaches and individuals providing them with the tools required to traverse the intricate terrain of coaching with wisdom, empathy, and purpose.

Radiate boundless love towards the entire world.

– Buddha

Chapter 11
Elevate Your Coaching Game

In Chapter 11, we discuss the importance of personal development for coaches and how Buddhist principles and compassionate coaching can contribute to it. Apart from revisiting self-care, mindfulness practices for coaches and strategies for maintaining inner balance while supporting others, we will study the ethical responsibilities of coaching.

A Story That Highlights the Importance of Self-Care:

In ancient Japan, there was a renowned Zen monastery led by a wise and compassionate master named Sōen. Many monks gathered at the monastery seeking his spiritual guidance and enlightenment.

One day, a young and enthusiastic monk approached Master Sōen and said, "Master, I am dedicated to my practice. I meditate diligently, study scriptures, and strive to serve others. But lately, I feel overwhelmed and exhausted. I don't know how to find balance."

Master Sōen listened attentively and then asked, "Have you ever observed the tea ceremony?"

The monk was puzzled but nodded in response.

The master smiled and said, "During the tea ceremony, the host prepares tea with utmost care and attention. They pay attention to every movement, every gesture and every breath. But there is one thing they never forget—to drink the tea themselves."

The young monk's eyes widened with realization.

Master Sōen continued, "Just like the tea ceremony, your practice should include self-care. It is not selfish to take care of yourself—it is essential. When you are depleted, how can you truly serve others?"

The young monk bowed deeply, grateful for the wisdom bestowed upon him by his master. From that day forward, he integrated self-care practices into his daily routine. He made time for quiet contemplation, engaged in activities that brought him joy, and nourished his body and mind with wholesome food and rest.

As the monk began self-care, he found a renewed sense of balance and clarity. His meditation became more joyful with better concentration, and his interactions with others became more compassionate and authentic. By taking care of himself, he became an inspiration to fellow monks and a source of support and guidance.

This Zen story reminds us that self-care is not a luxury but an integral part of our spiritual journey. Just as the tea ceremony host takes time to enjoy the tea, we too must prioritize our well-being and nurture ourselves.

It is crucial to acknowledge the necessary prerequisite for growth. Just as a sturdy foundation is necessary for a magnificent edifice, personal development forms the bedrock upon which a coach's journey unfolds. Coaching is not just about supporting the growth and development of clients. It also involves the ongoing self-improvement and thriving of the coach. Therefore, it is imperative that we never lose sight of our progress and evolution in the process. The coach's personal advancement is essential for maintaining competence, expanding his capacity to serve clients and deepening his understanding of human behaviour and change processes.

In Mahāyāna Buddhism, the concept of self-care is intricately connected to the teachings of compassion and mindfulness. Here are a few concepts from Mahāyāna Buddhism that encompass elements of self-care:

1. ***Bodhicitta***: This term refers to the awakened mind of compassion and the aspiration to attain enlightenment for the benefit of all beings. A *bodhicitta* involves developing a deep sense of care and compassion for oneself and others.

2. ***Upaya***: *Upaya*, often translated as *skilful means*, refers to the use of various methods and practices to placate suffering and promote

well-being. This concept encourages individuals to adopt strategies for self-care, considering their unique needs and circumstances.

These *Mahayana* Buddhist practices accentuate the importance of self-care as a vital part of the path towards awakening and benefitting others.

A compelling real-life case study highlighting the importance of self-care is the story of Arianna Huffington, the co-founder of *The Huffington Post*.[76]

During the early years of building *The Huffington Post*, Arianna Huffington was renowned for her tireless work ethic and unwavering commitment to her career. She pushed herself relentlessly, often sacrificing sleep and neglecting her well-being in her quest for success. However, a pivotal moment occurred in 2007 that changed everything.

One fateful day, Arianna experienced a severe episode of exhaustion and burnout. She collapsed, hitting her head on her desk and sustaining an injury. This incident served as a critical wake-up call, which compelled her to reassess her priorities and recognize the critical importance of placing self-care at the top.

Following this transformative event, Arianna became a passionate advocate for self-care, thus implementing substantial changes in her life. She took up mindfulness practices, included regular exercise into her routine and made sleep a non-negotiable priority. Additionally, she consciously established boundaries, disconnecting from technology and creating a clear delineation between work and personal life.

Arianna's personal journey and her commitment to self-care had a ripple effect, which led to a cultural transformation within *The Huffington Post*. She introduced comprehensive wellness programmes and initiatives for employees, which underscored the implication of self-care and achieving a harmonious work-life balance.

Through her experiences and the positive changes, which she introduced within her organization, Arianna Huffington emerged as a prominent influencer in the realm of self-care. She authored books, such as *Thrive* and delivered inspiring speeches, which encourage individuals and companies to celebrate self-care as a cornerstone of success and fulfilment.

The case of Arianna Huffington serves as a compelling testament, highlighting the fundamental role that self-care plays in both personal and professional spheres. It exemplifies how leaders who prioritize their well-being can inspire others to do the same, which ultimately leads to healthier and more sustainable work environments.

Here are some key points highlighting the importance of self-care for coaches:

1. **Enhanced Self-awareness**: We have already discussed in detail the monumental impact of self-care. By investing in themselves, coaches are able to clearly decipher their values, beliefs, strengths and limitations. It is only by looking within that one can increase self-awareness, which is crucial for building authentic relationships with clients, managing biases and maintaining objectivity. A coach who engages in such inner work through previously mentioned practices, such as journaling, mindfulness meditation or attending self-reflection workshops can have a better grasp of their triggers.

   In *The Mindful Coach* by Doug Silsbee, a prominent author in the coaching field, the importance of mindfulness and self-awareness for coaches is highlighted. This book points out how coaches can enhance their effectiveness with mindfulness practices as a major part of their daily routines.[77]

2. **Expanded Perspectives**: Dedicating quality time for oneself broadens the coach's perspectives and widens his lens of perception. It exposes him to diverse ideas, philosophies, and approaches, thus enabling him to think more creatively and flexibly when working with clients. This expanded perspective augments his ability to really facilitate meaningful change.

A coach should thus actively seek out diverse learning opportunities, such as attending conferences, participating in cross-disciplinary workshops or studying different cultural practices.

3. **Emotional Intelligence and Empathy**: A coach devotes effort for a thriving self through emotional intelligence training or participating in experiential exercises that deepen his understanding of emotions. As a result, the coach becomes more attuned to subtle emotional cues both of himself and from clients, thus allowing them to respond with empathy and compassion. This heightened emotional intelligence strengthens the coaching relationship.

4. **Continuous Growth**: By prioritizing their development, coaches demonstrate a commitment to their profession and model the importance of lifelong learning to their clients. This ensures the coach stays updated with the latest coaching methodologies, research and best practices, and enables them to provide high-quality coaching services to their clients. Coaches thus stay relevant in a rapidly evolving field.

5. **Role Modelling and Authenticity**: Personal development allows coaches to embody the principles and values that they advocate, making them more authentic and credible in their coaching relationships. Coaches who consistently engage in enriching their lives and practice inspire clients to do the same. This inspires clients to embrace their growth too and demonstrates that self-progress is a lifelong process.

6. **Professional Ethics and Boundaries**: A coach regularly engages themselves in activities related to ethical decision-making, such as attending ethics workshops or seeking supervision from experienced coaches [discussed in detail later]. These activities help the coaches clarify their values, establish appropriate boundaries and navigate complex ethical dilemmas that may arise during coaching engagements, which ensures that they operate with integrity and adhere to professional standards.

By spotlighting their well-being, coaches not only build their professional skills and effectiveness but also expand their understanding of the human experience. This allows them to bring their best selves to the coaching relationship, aiding transformative experiences for their clients.

There are more anecdotes of great leaders and CEOs prioritizing self-care. Here are a few examples:

1. Jeff Weiner, the former CEO of LinkedIn, is known for giving prominence to mindfulness and compassion in the workplace. He introduced programmes, such as Compassion Week, where employees were encouraged to practice genuine acts of kindness and self-care that go on to become a regular practice and way of life.[78]

2. Bill Gates, the co-founder of Microsoft, is known for his commitment to taking regular *think weeks*. During these weeks, Gates disconnects from his usual work routine to reflect, read, and rejuvenate. This practice allows him to recharge and gain fresh perspectives.[79]

3. Indra Nooyi, the former CEO of PepsiCo, has spoken about the importance of self-care and work-life balance. She encouraged employees to take care of their personal well-being and often shared personal anecdotes about how she prioritized her health and family life.[80]

These anecdotes highlight that even highly successful leaders and CEOs recognize the value of self-care and give it primacy in their lives. Their examples spur coaches and individuals in leadership positions to put their well-being at the top while pursuing their professional goals.

Some Ways to Work on Personal Development:

1. **Reflective Practice:** Coaches can set aside dedicated time for journaling about their coaching sessions, reflecting on their experiences and working on areas for improvement. They can also use self-assessment tools, such as

the *Coaching Competency Assessment* by the International Coach Federation (ICF) to evaluate their coaching skills and identify areas for growth.

2. **Continuous Learning**: Coaches can attend workshops or conferences related to coaching. For example, they can participate in the **World Business and Executive Coach Summit** or enrol in advanced coaching programmes, such as the *Co-active Professional Coach Training* offered by the Coaches Training Institute (CTI).

3. **Supervision and Mentoring**: Coaches can seek supervision or mentoring from experienced coaches or join supervision groups. The European Mentoring and Coaching Council (EMCC) offers a list of qualified supervisors and mentors for coaches to connect with.

4. **Personal Therapy or Coaching**: Coaches can go for therapy or coaching to deepen their self-awareness and take a look at any personal challenges that may impact their coaching practice. They can work with a therapist or coach who specializes in working with helping professionals.

5. **Peer Support and Networking**: Coaches can join coaching associations such as the ICF, Association for Coaching (AC) or International Association of Coaching (IAC) to connect with peers. They can also participate in online communities, such as the **Coaching Tools and Techniques** group or be a part of coaching meetups in their local chapter/area.

6. **Mindfulness and Self-care**: Coaches can incorporate mindfulness practices into their daily routine, such as *meditation* or *mindful breathing*. They can also aim at self-care activities, such as regular exercise, spending time in nature or partaking in hobbies that bring them rest and act as breathers.

7. **Feedback and Evaluation**: Coaches can actively seek feedback from their clients by using feedback forms or conducting regular check-ins to assess the effectiveness of their coaching. They can also go for formal

evaluations, such as the ICF's *Coach Knowledge Assessment* or the AC's *Coach Accreditation Process* to attain a thorough grasp of the concepts while pursuing the next level of coaching competencies.

By implementing these strategies, coaches can maintain their equipoise while providing support to others.

At the same time, coaches must also involve themselves in personal development to honour their **ethical responsibilities** in coaching through various approaches. Here are some insights:

1. **Attend Ethical Training Workshops**: Coaches can participate in workshops or training programmes that provide a structured learning environment to examine ethical challenges, discuss case studies and develop strategies for upholding ethical standards in coaching relationships. It also allows coaches to network with peers and learn from their experiences.

2. **Reflect on Ethical Principles**: Supervision provides a safe and confidential space for coaches to reflect on their coaching practice when it comes to ethics and standards.

3. **Practice Ethical Decision-making**: Personal development should include honing skills in ethical decision-making. Coaches can engage in discussions to improve their ability to make principled and responsible choices in challenging coaching situations. This proactive approach prepares coaches to handle ethical impasses effectively and fittingly.

By keeping ethical responsibilities at the forefront, coaches can ensure that their coaching relationships are built on professionalism.

Self-care has gained significant recognition and importance globally, especially in the context of well-being and professional performance.

Numerous studies and reputable sources have highlighted the significance of self-care practices:

1. The World Health Organization (WHO) acknowledges the importance of self-care for maintaining and promoting health. They have developed a framework for self-care interventions that empower individuals to take an active role in their health, especially in coping with chronic conditions and preventive care.

2. Research published in the *Journal of Occupational and Environmental Medicine* has shown that self-care practices, such as regular exercise, sufficient sleep and stress management, positively impact employees' productivity and overall welfare in the workplace.[81]

3. A study conducted by Deloitte found that organizations that give precedence to employee well-being and provide resources for self-care experience higher employee engagement, reduced absenteeism and better performance in general.[82]

4. In the coaching field, the International Coach Federation (ICF) recognizes the importance of self-care for coaches. The ICF acknowledges that coaches need to attend to their health to be more effective in supporting their clients.

5. The American Psychological Association (APA) advocates for self-care as a crucial component of mental health. They recommend self-care practices, such as seeking social support, taking up hobbies, and maintaining work-life balance to boost psychological resilience and reduce burnout.[83]

6. Universities and healthcare institutions have made self-care education a part of their programmes to equip students and professionals with tools to handle stress, improve work-life balance and prevent burnout.

Overall, the growing body of research and recognition is bending heavily towards *health first* approach.

Conclusion:

Glamorization of busyness, often associated with a hectic lifestyle and constant hustle has detrimental effects on individuals' health and well-being. In modern society, being busy is often seen as a status symbol, where one's worth is measured by their packed schedule and ability to multitask. However, this culture of busyness can lead to several negative consequences. It can blur the boundaries between work and personal life, which makes it challenging for individuals to disconnect and recharge. People may delay seeking medical attention or ignore warning signs of health issues due to their demanding schedules, which leads to more significant health problems down the line.

Thus, to address these challenges, it is essential to shift the narrative surrounding busyness and prioritize the importance of self-care. Highlighting the value of rest, relaxation, and mindfulness can help individuals lead healthier lives. Hailing a culture that values quality over quantity can lead to improved health outcomes and a more sustainable approach to life and work.

Let us close the chapter with some thoughts on love from Thich Nhat Hanh's ***How to Love*** from his ***Mindfulness Essentials*** series.

"Once you know how to come home to yourself, then you can open your home to other people because you have something to offer. The other person has to do exactly the same thing if they are to have something to offer you. Otherwise, they will have nothing to share but their loneliness, sickness and suffering. This can't help heal you at all."

The more we focus on our self-care, the richer the gifts of presence
and kindness we shall give to others.

– Buddha

Breakthrough Beyond Barriers

In Chapter 12, we delve into the typical obstacles and difficulties faced by coaches—situations they may encounter in their coaching practice—and discover strategies to overcome them. This chapter addresses topics, such as handling resistance, being adept at difficult conversations and surmounting self-doubt.

Deriving from a **Zen proverb**, the phrase, *the obstacle is the path* refers to the idea that no obstacle can be negotiated just by avoidance. You must tackle it head-on to move ahead.

This school of thought insists that hindrances actually present opportunities for improvement. Prevailing over trying circumstances can make us stronger, more resolute and more robust. Choosing the *easy* way out stops us from embracing and tackling challenges.

The Zen mindset is all about taking control of the choices in our lives, and one of the most crucial choices we can make is to face these barriers rather than sidestepping them.

Writer and creative director Darnell Lamont Walker says, "Sometimes our walls exist just to see who has the strength to knock them down."

By being flexible, courageous and resilient, we can turn impediments into the most crucial part of the journey.

Koans

These are specific types of puzzles or paradoxical statements used in Zen practice to provoke deep contemplation and perceptiveness. They are time and again presented as questions or statements that often defy logical reasoning.

They push practitioners to transcend dualistic thinking and can help surpass seemingly unsurmountable situations. The purpose of a *koan* is not to provide a straightforward answer but rather to provoke a shift in consciousness and open the door to direct realization. Many practitioners spend significant time meditating on a *koan*, thus allowing it to penetrate their awareness and guide them towards a direct experience of truth.

Here is a classic Zen *koan* for you:

"Two hands clap and there is a sound; what is the sound of one hand?"

This *koan*, often attributed to Zen master, Hakuin Ekaku, challenges the practitioner to investigate the nature of sound, duality, and the concept of one-hand clapping. It urges the practitioner to move beyond intellectual reasoning and seek direct experiential understanding. The *koan* serves as a catalyst for breaking through habitual patterns of thinking and perceiving reality.

The above-mentioned Zen *koan* can be related to overcoming challenges in coaching practice in the following ways:

1. **Contesting Dualistic Thinking**: In coaching, practitioners often encounter situations that seem paradoxical or contradictory. The *koan* encourages coaches to question binary thinking and fixed perspectives. By acceptance of a more fluid and non-dualistic approach, coaches can look out for alternative solutions, perspectives, and possibilities.

2. **Adopting Silence and Stillness**: The *koan* invites contemplation and reflection, thus stressing the importance of silence and stillness in gaining insights. Coaches can apply this principle for their clients to pause, reflect, and connect with their inner wisdom. By providing a quiet and receptive environment, coaches can help clients access their answers.

3. **Developing Non-attachment**: The *koan* reminds us to avoid rushing for quick answers or seeking validation from others. Similarly, in coaching, clients can be encouraged to let go of rigid expectations and

outcomes making room for viewing possibilities openly, and bringing in adaptability and strength when facing hurdles.

4. **Dwelling in Paradoxical Inquiry**: The *koan* presents a question that defies conventional logic and calls for a deeper inquiry beyond rational thinking. Coaches can apply this approach by inviting clients to consider paradoxes and contradictions within their challenges. This can lead to breakthroughs that may not be accessible through linear problem-solving approaches.

5. **Embracing the Unanswerable**: The *koan's* question itself is unanswerable in a conventional sense. Coaches can draw inspiration from this by stepping into the unknown and acknowledging that not all challenges have clear-cut solutions. By choosing to walk through uncertainty, coaches can help clients.

Scenarios

Client 1

Imagine a coach working with a client named Aisha who is facing a career dilemma. Aisha has been working in a stable but unfulfilling job for many years. Recently, she has discovered a new career path that aligns with her passions and values, but it comes with more uncertainty and potential risks.

As Aisha discusses her situation with the coach, she expresses fears and concerns about leaving her current job. She worries about financial stability, the opinions of others and the potential challenges of starting a new career from scratch. These fears create resistance and hold her back from pursuing her true calling.

Inspired by a Zen *koan*, the coach asks her to reflect on what it would feel like to stay in her current job and what it would feel like to pursue a new career path.

Through this inquiry, Aisha realizes that staying in her current job might provide stability, but it also perpetuates her unhappiness and stifles her growth. On the other hand, taking up the new career path brings excitement, contentment, and alignment with her passions.

As the coaching conversations progress, the coach helps Aisha chalk out probable risks associated with the new career path and the best way forward. They discuss ways to build a support network, create a financial plan, and develop the necessary skills and knowledge to succeed.

During the coaching process, Aisha connects with her intuition and inner guidance. In these moments, Aisha discovers a newfound courage to step out of her comfort zone. As Aisha continues to work with the coach, she rejoices that sometimes there is no absolute right or wrong choice. Instead of looking for a definitive answer, she concentrates on moving forward and recognizes that choosing a new career path involves taking calculated risks.

With the coach's help, Aisha gains the confidence to make a decision. She decides to leave her current job. While she acknowledges that the road ahead will not be smooth, she feels a sense of liberation and excitement for the future.

Client 2:

Imagine a client who is contemplating whether to start a successful business or continue working in a corporate job.

The coach invites the client to reflect on the following questions:

- How might success be defined for you beyond financial gains? What other factors are important to consider?

- Can you find a middle ground that combines your entrepreneurial aspirations with the stability and benefits of your current job?

- What creative solutions or alternative paths can you think of to strike a balance between following your passion and maintaining security?

- What steps can you take to mitigate risks and build a solid foundation for your business venture?

Without providing direct advice or solutions, the coach kindles the thinking of the client, who decides to conduct market research and understand the nuances of entrepreneurs who have successfully transitioned from a corporate career to entrepreneurship. The coach partners with the client in assessing risks, developing a business plan and identifying promising support networks.

Accepting the paradoxes and contradictions that arise, the client is inspired to find their unique path, considering both their aspirations and practical considerations. By amalgamating the Zen *koans* principles into the coaching approach, the coach helps the client overcome their resistance to change. The client then goes on to find confidence in their decision-making.

Coaching Obstacles: Strategies for Coaches at Any Stage

1. Resistance:

Connect with coachees by building rapport, trust and emphasizing the benefits of coaching.

Example: Research shows that coaching participants who understand the value of coaching are more likely to be motivated and actively participate in the process.

One notable example of a global leader who initially had resistance to coaching but eventually changed his perspective is Satya Nadella, the CEO of Microsoft.

When Satya Nadella took over as CEO of Microsoft in 2014, he inherited a company which was facing significant challenges. However, he was initially sceptical about the role of coaching in his leadership journey. Nadella believed that coaching might impede his ability to make independent decisions and hinder him.

However, as Nadella began to face the complex demands of leading a global technology giant, he recognized the value of asking for support. He realized that coaching could bring in fresh perspectives, bolster his leadership skills and help him be the leader he envisioned to be.

Nadella's change of heart led him to actively participate in executive coaching. Through coaching, his leadership style became clearer to him. Nadella's willingness to take up coaching has been credited as a significant factor in Microsoft's successful transformation during his tenure.

Satya Nadella's coach during his transformational journey as CEO of Microsoft was Bill Campbell, a renowned executive coach and former CEO of Intuit. Bill Campbell, often referred to as *The Coach of Silicon Valley* was known for his influential coaching relationships with many prominent leaders in the tech industry.

Satya Nadella has publicly acknowledged the momentous influence of Bill Campbell on his leadership journey. Nadella has stressed the importance of having a trusted adviser and coach who can offer an outside perspective.

The example of Satya Nadella serves as a testament to the transformative power of coaching—even for seasoned leaders. It brings to light the importance of being open regardless of one's initial reservations.

2. Self-awareness:

Utilize assessment tools, introspective exercises and expert questioning to help coachees discern their strengths and areas for development.

Example: Studies have found that increased self-awareness leads to improved performance and personal growth in coaching.

One leading example of a global CEO who has exhibited a commitment to augmenting self-awareness is Sundar Pichai, the CEO of Google and Alphabet Inc., who has spoken about the importance of self-awareness in various interviews and public appearances.

Here's how:

a) **Growth and Adaptability**: Pichai has underscored the value of taking feedback from others as a means to continuously evolve. He is a strong advocate of open and honest communication within the company, both from employees and external stakeholders. By actively listening to feedback and considering different perspectives, Pichai shows a willingness to learn and adapt.

b) **Clear Vision and Focus**: Pichai has acknowledged the benefits of mindfulness and meditation in his personal life. He has expressed how these practices help him maintain unwavering concentration, and clarity of mind and aid in better decision-making. Pichai demonstrates a commitment to self-reflection and inner balance through this.

c) **The Power of Human Connection**: Pichai appreciates the importance of empathy in leadership. He accentuates the need to connect with people on a human level. Pichai's empathy-driven approach reflects his awareness of the bearing leaders can have on the morale and happiness of their teams.

d) **Curiosity and Intellectual Development**: Pichai is known for his insatiable curiosity and passion for knowledge. He encourages Googlers to pursue continuous learning of new ideas, and be on the look-out for intellectual challenges. This is proof of his belief in and awareness of the power of self-improvement.

e) **Balancing Ambition and Humility**: Pichai strikes a balance between ambitious goals and humble leadership. He acknowledges the collective efforts of the Google team and credits them for the company's success. Pichai's humility highlights his self-awareness and recognition of the contributions of others.

By exemplifying these qualities and practices, Sundar Pichai has become an influential figure in the tech industry and beyond. His focus serves as an inspiration for coaches, clients and leaders.

3. Time Management:

Collaborate with coachees to identify time management strategies and set realistic goals that fit their busy schedules.

Example: Virtual coaching sessions and leveraging technology offer flexible options, thus allowing coachees to integrate coaching into their demanding routines.

One foremost example of a global CEO who has effectively managed time is Tim Cook, the CEO of Apple Inc. Known for his disciplined approach and attention to detail, Cook has been praised for his exceptional time management skills.

Cook's commitment to time management is evident in his daily routine. He is known for starting his day early, often waking up before 4:00 a.m., which allows him to have dedicated time for exercise, reading, and planning. By prioritizing his mornings, Cook sets the tone for a productive day ahead.

Furthermore, Cook has embraced technology to optimize his time management. He is often seen utilizing Apple's productivity tools, such as the Calendar and Notes applications, to keep track of his schedule, set reminders, and organize his tasks. By leveraging technology, Cook streamlines his workflow and stays organized, which allows him to make the most of his valuable time.

Cook believes that time is a precious resource and treats it with the utmost respect. One aspect of Cook's time management approach is his focus on delegation. As the CEO of a global company, such as Apple, Cook is fully cognisant of the importance of empowering and trusting his team. He delegates tasks and responsibilities to capable individuals, which allows him to concentrate on high-level strategic decisions and critical matters.

Moreover, Cook's time management practices extend beyond his daily routine. He has implemented company-wide initiatives at Apple to optimize productivity and efficiency. For example, he introduced *quiet hours* during certain periods of the week, where employees are urged to stay engrossed in individual work without interruptions from meetings or emails.

Cook's dedication to time management is also seen in his commitment to punctuality. He is known for being prompt and expects the same from others. This emphasis on punctuality helps ensure that meetings and engagements start and end on time, thus maximizing efficiency and avoiding unnecessary delays.

The broader principles of time management and its importance in professional success have a strong empirical foundation. Coaches can draw upon this research and adapt these evidence-based principles to their practice and personal progression.

4. Accountability:

Clearly define expectations, establish measurable goals and regularly check in with coachees to further accountability, where they take ownership of their actions.

Example: Research indicates that accountability structures, such as regular progress check-ins, significantly contribute to goal attainment and behaviour change.

A prominent example of a global CEO who exemplifies the trait of establishing accountability is Alan Mulally, the former CEO of Ford Motor Company. Mulally is credited with successfully turning around the struggling automaker during his tenure.

Under Mulally's leadership, a weekly meeting called the business plan review (BPR), was implemented where executives from different departments would come together to review progress and discuss any challenges. This meeting served as a platform for open and transparent communication, which brought in a culture of accountability throughout the organization.

One key aspect of Mulally's approach to instituting accountability was the implementation of a colour-coded system known as the red-yellow-green (RYG) status. During the BPR meetings, each executive would present their department's progress using a simple visual representation of their performance.

Green indicated that everything was on track, yellow represented areas of concern and red signified significant challenges or issues.

By using this system, Mulally created a culture of transparency and accountability, where executives were encouraged to freely discuss challenges and collaborate on finding solutions. The RYG status allowed for a quick assessment of the organization's overall health and highlighted areas that needed attention.

This approach had a substantial impact on Ford's performance and culture. It helped to break down silos and ensure that everyone was accountable for their respective roles and responsibilities. Mulally's stress on accountability played a crucial role in Ford's successful turnaround and return to profitability.

While specific data or quotes regarding the impact of Alan Mulally's accountability practices are not available, the success of Ford under his leadership speaks to the effectiveness of his approach. Ford's financial performance improved significantly during his tenure, and the company regained its position as a leading player in the automotive industry.

The example of Alan Mulally showcases the importance of establishing accountability as a leadership trait. It demonstrates how a CEO's commitment can create a high-performance culture and drive positive outcomes.

5. Emotional Blocks and Resistance to Change:

Establish a supportive environment for coachees.

Example: Emotional intelligence training for coaches enhances their ability to address emotional barriers and support coachees in their transformation.

One exemplary case of a global CEO who effectively addressed emotional blocks and resistance to change is Jeff Bezos, the renowned founder and former CEO of Amazon. Throughout his journey, Bezos encountered numerous difficulties and encountered resistance from within the organization.

In one remarkable instance, Bezos met with scepticism and defiance while introducing the concept of Amazon Prime, a subscription service that offered fast shipping and various benefits to members. Despite initial doubts, Bezos remained committed to his vision and persevered in rising above emotional blocks and resistance.

He initiated a meeting with the team responsible for the project and presented them with an empty chair, thus representing the importance of the customer. Bezos passionately shared customer testimonials and stories and underscored the likely impact and value of Amazon Prime. This approach helped to bridge the emotional gap and ignite enthusiasm within the team.

Bezos also utilized data to support his arguments and decision-making. He shared statistical evidence which confirmed the increasing demand for faster shipping and the prospective market size for such a service. By combining compelling anecdotes and substantive facts, Bezos effectively allayed fears around the new service and led the successful launch of Amazon Prime.

The results speak for themselves. Amazon Prime has become a monumental success and boasts of having millions of loyal subscribers worldwide. It revolutionized the e-commerce landscape and solidified Amazon's position as a market leader. The growth of Amazon Prime serves as a testament to Bezos' ability to resolve disagreements, leverage emotional intelligence, and drive organizational change.

6. Resource Limitations:

Assist coachees in identifying available resources, networking opportunities, and relevant training programmes to maximize their growth potential.

Example: Encouraging coachees to connect with mentors or professionals in their field expands their network and provides access to valuable resources and guidance.

A striking example of a global CEO who effectively beat resource limitations and leveraged available resources and networking opportunities is Elon Musk, the CEO of Tesla and SpaceX. Musk's entrepreneurial journey is characterized by his ability to sail across tough circumstances and make the most of limited resources.

In the early years of Tesla and SpaceX, Musk faced significant financial constraints and resource limitations. However, he showed remarkable resourcefulness by actively seeking out partnerships, alliances, and funding opportunities. One notable instance is the collaboration between Tesla and Daimler, a multinational automotive corporation. Through this strategic partnership, Tesla got access to Daimler's resources, including engineering expertise and capital investment, which contributed considerably to Tesla's meteoric rise.

In addition to his association with Daimler, Elon Musk's partnership with NASA has been a weighty factor in prevailing over resource limitations. SpaceX, under Musk's leadership, has established a fruitful relationship with NASA, the National Aeronautics and Space Administration of the United States.

Such contracts and connections with NASA have proven to be valuable for SpaceX. For instance, SpaceX's involvement with NASA's Commercial Crew Programme has allowed the company to develop crewed space capsules, such as the Crew Dragon, and deliver supplies to the International Space Station. These associations have not only provided SpaceX with monetary assistance but have also bolstered its credibility and capabilities in the aerospace industry.

Publicly available accounts and reports bring to the fore the fruitful impact of SpaceX and NASA joining hands, including milestones achieved in crewed spaceflight and ground-breaking achievements in rocket technology. All this has not only benefited SpaceX but has also contributed to advancing NASA's space exploration objectives.

The evidence of Musk's resourcefulness and networking prowess can be seen in the impressive growth of Tesla and SpaceX. By studying Musk's approach, one can learn valuable lessons about identifying and utilizing available resources, initiating partnerships with key stakeholders and capitalizing on networking opportunities. Applying these strategies can help coaches, clients, and leaders alike.

7. Self-doubt:

The first step is to be aware of self-doubt and acknowledge its presence. Understand that self-doubt is a normal part of the coaching journey and that even skilful coaches may experience it at times. Separate yourself from self-doubt and view it objectively. Defy these thoughts by questioning their validity and looking at alternative perspectives. Set realistic expectations for yourself and your coaching practice. Embrace the learning process and understand that self-doubt can be an opportunity for growth.

Example: A remarkable example of a contemporary world leader who openly recognized and admitted to self-doubt is Jacinda Ardern, the Prime Minister of New Zealand. Ardern's leadership during challenging times, such as the Christchurch Mosque shootings and the COVID-19 pandemic, has been extensively praised. Despite her achievements, she has been open about moments of vulnerability, which has resonated with many people around the world.

In various public accounts and interviews, Ardern has shared her experiences of the internal struggles she faces as a leader. She has discussed the pressure to make difficult decisions, the weight of public expectations and the constant self-evaluation that comes with leadership. By doing so, Ardern has shown a genuine and relatable side of leadership and has broken the perception of leaders as infallible figures.

The evidence of Ardern's self-doubt lies not only in her public statements but also in her actions and leadership style. Despite her moments of uncertainty, she has consistently displayed resilience, empathy, and determination in addressing critical issues. Her ability to focus on the well-being of her people has earned her widespread admiration.

Public opinion polls and surveys also reveal the positive perception of Ardern's leadership, which further supports the evidence of her effectiveness as a leader. Her high approval ratings and the appreciation she has received globally for her handling of crises underline the impact of her leadership approach.

Jacinda Ardern's example serves as an important reminder that self-doubt does not diminish one's ability to lead effectively. Instead, it humanizes leaders and leads to a deeper connection with the public. Leaders, such as Ardern portray humility, authenticity and the willingness to continually grow and learn through this demeanour which discards putting up a façade to seem super-human-like.

The case of Jacinda Ardern provides invaluable understanding for coaches, clients and leaders alike. It emphatically tells us to accept vulnerability rather than suppress or deny it.

By seamlessly presenting these strategies and incorporating evidence-based data and examples, readers of all backgrounds and experience levels can glean valuable insights to overcome obstacles and achieve success.

Here is a famous poem by Robert Frost that eloquently captures the idea of life's challenges and the decisions we face.

It aptly summarises the chapter:

The Road Not Taken by Robert Frost

Two roads diverged in a yellow wood,
And sorry I could not travel both,
And be one traveller, long I stood,

And looked down one as far as I could,

To where it bent in the undergrowth;

Then took the other, as just as fair,

And having perhaps the better claim,

Because it was grassy and wanted wear;

Though as for that the passing there,

Had worn them really about the same,

And both that morning equally lay,

In leaves no step had trodden black.

Oh, I kept the first for another day!

Yet knowing how way leads on to way,

I doubted if I should ever come back.

I shall be telling this with a sigh,

Somewhere ages and ages hence:

Two roads diverged in a wood, and I—

I took the one less travelled by,

And that has made all the difference.

This poem reflects the dilemmas we encounter when faced with options and the uncertainty of not knowing which path to take. It brings to attention the fear of making the wrong decision and the possible regret that may follow. The barriers in this context are the different paths that we can choose, each with its own set of unknowns and impending consequences.

The poem invites us to contemplate the ordeals we face in life and the paths we choose. It reminds us that taking the road less travelled, though mired with fear of the unknown can lead to amazing growth and life-altering experiences.

Let us conclude our discussion with a brilliant example from nature on overcoming challenges:

The pistol shrimp, also known as the snapping shrimp, is a small but fascinating creature found in oceans around the world. Despite its size, this tiny shrimp possesses a unique and powerful weapon to deal with threats.

The pistol shrimp has one oversized claw that it uses as a formidable tool. When threatened or in need of food, it contracts its claw and releases it with incredible speed and creates a cavitation bubble. The collapse of this bubble produces a loud snapping sound and a powerful shockwave that stuns or immobilizes its prey.

What makes the pistol shrimp's ability noteworthy is that the speed at which its claw snaps creates temperatures comparable to the surface of the sun for a split second. This phenomenon is called supercavitation and allows the shrimp to break through even the toughest shells or rocks.

The pistol shrimp's extraordinary adaptation serves as a metaphor for tackling life's tribulations. Like the shrimp, we may face struggles that seem insurmountable. However, by drawing inspiration from the pistol shrimp's resilience and resourcefulness, we can find unique ways to defeat hurdles.

The lesson from the pistol shrimp is twofold.

First, it reminds us of the importance of adaptability and leveraging our strengths. The shrimp utilizes its specialized claw to its advantage, thus demonstrating that sometimes unconventional approaches can yield extraordinary results.

Second, the pistol shrimp's ability to create something powerful out of seemingly small means teaches us the value of perspective. It highlights that even when faced with limited resources or unfavourable circumstances, we have the ability to make a lasting impact.

By learning from the pistol shrimp, we can approach our distresses with inventiveness and a rebounding spirit and emerge stronger on the other side.

As we analyse the principles and learnings in this book, it is important to know that while the focus is on coaching, the learnings, particularly from this chapter with experiences and lessons from CEOs and world leaders are highly applicable to the training and facilitation industry and individuals wanting to climb the corporate ladder. Here is how they can be effectively integrated into training programmes and resonate with all individuals:

1. **Inspirational Stories**: These stories of triumph and resoluteness go beyond coaching and can inspire trainees in the training industry. They validate the power of self-care and embracing self-belief. Such narratives motivate individuals to push themselves beyond their limits and strive for excellence.

2. **Practical Strategies**: The strategies employed by successful individuals are transferable across various domains. Techniques for effective goal setting, time management, building support networks, and utilizing technology can be customized to suit the needs of trainers and individuals.

3. **Skill Development**: The skills that contribute to success are not limited to coaching alone. Effective communication, emotional intelligence, adaptability, problem-solving, and decision-making are essential skills for trainers and individuals in any professional field. Incorporating these skill-building exercises into training programmes ensures their practical applicability.

4. **Cultivating Resilience**: Resilience is crucial for everyone in the face of setbacks and trying times in life. By introducing resilience-building techniques, such as mindset shifts training programmes, trainers can equip individuals with the tools needed to bounce back from adversity and thrive in their endeavours.

5. **Role Modelling**: Accomplished individuals serve as role models regardless of the industry. Their qualities of empathy, authenticity, inclusivity, and integrity are universally relevant. Trainers can introduce these qualities to stir participants to embody ethical conduct and social responsibility in their practices and professional interactions.

6. **Application in Real Life**: The book's insights are not confined to coaching sessions alone. By facilitating discussions and interactive exercises, trainers can guide participants to reflect on how the lessons learned can be applied in their everyday lives. This bridge between

training and real-life application augments the relevance and effectiveness of the programme.

In summary, while the book and this chapter focus on coaching, the principles and learnings it presents hold great value for all. Trainers and facilitators particularly can create impactful programmes based on them to thrive in their professional pursuits.

Conclusion:

Chapter 12 has shown that coaching obstacles are not roadblocks but part of the path to growth. By confronting challenges directly, we become stronger and more determined. The Buddhist mindset reminds us to take control of our choices, especially when facing barriers. Success comes when we're flexible, courageous, and resilient, turning impediments into springboards for happiness.

No one saves us but ourselves. No one can and no one may.
We ourselves must walk the path.

– Buddha

Chapter 13

Deepening the Client-Coach Relationship

Do you have a strong desire to feel heard, validated, and understood?

We all have!

As social beings, humans have always relied on interpersonal connections for survival and well-being. In the Palaeolithic era, strong relationships were crucial for protection, cooperation and the exchange of resources. Our brain's social circuitry developed in response to these needs, and the longing for deep connections remains ingrained in our psychological makeup.

The need for these deep relationships has evolved even more over millennia as humans have progressed and adapted to changing environments. While the core desire for connection and belonging remains consistent, the expression and fulfilment of this need have undergone significant transformations. Let us see how:

1. **Social Structures**: In early human history, small hunter-gatherer groups formed the basis of social organization. These tight-knit communities relied on strong interpersonal bonds for survival and sustenance. As human societies transitioned to agricultural settlements and later to complex civilizations, social structures became more elaborate, encompassing larger communities, extended families and social hierarchies. The need for deep relationships expanded to accommodate these ever-changing social structures.

2. **Technological Advancements**: The development of language, written communication and transportation expanded the possibilities for connection and facilitated the formation of broader social networks. The invention of writing systems, for example, enabled people to

communicate and form relationships across great distances and different cultures. The advent of modern transportation and communication technologies, such as telephones, the internet and social media, further accelerated the reach and speed of human connections.

3. **Cultural Influences**: Cultural norms and values have shaped the expression of the need for deep relationships. Different societies have emphasized varying forms of social interaction, such as extended family networks, community-oriented living or individualistic pursuits. These cultural influences have a bearing on the expectations and dynamics of relationships, which impacts how individuals seek and maintain connections with others.

4. **Psychological and Emotional Well-being**: Over time, humans have come to appreciate the immense impact of deep relationships on psychological and emotional well-being. Research in psychology and neuroscience has shown that social connection is essential for overall mental health and contributes to vitality, happiness, and a sense of purpose.

5. **Modern Challenges**: While the need for deep relationships remains innate, modern challenges, such as urbanization, globalization, and the fast-paced nature of life have created new barriers to forming and maintaining meaningful connections. People may experience social isolation, loneliness, and disconnection in the face of busy schedules, technological distractions and fragmented communities. As a result, there is a growing recognition of the need to intentionally prioritize and invest in relationships that have depth for holistic well-being.

Today, despite the advancements of modern society, the basal need for deep relationships persists. We still seek emotional support, understanding and a sense of belonging. In the fields of therapy, counselling and coaching, practitioners tap into this innate longing for connection and use it as a powerful tool to facilitate healing, growth and self-actualization.

Welcome to Chapter 13 of our coaching journey, Ties that Transform: *Deepening the Client-Coach Relationship*. In this chapter, we study the great impact of connection and rapport in the coaching process. As coaches, we understand that the quality of the relationship that we cultivate with our clients lays the foundation for it all.

To complement the existing approaches, we inspect the importance of accountability structures that go beyond traditional goal setting. We probe the innovative methods for developing accountability, such as accountability partnerships, peer coaching circles and personalized accountability tools. These structures create a web of support that keeps our clients driven, enthused, and committed to their growth.

Join us in this chapter as we break free from conventional coaching paradigms and tread a daring path towards inner change, leaving no stone unturned in our quest to deepen the ties that shift something at the core of our lives.

So, let us with an open heart and an unwavering vow to be in the service of the client, read on.

We begin with a concept from Mesoamerican cultures related to relationship ties.

In Lak'ech: This concept comes from the Mayan civilization. *In Lak'ech* is a phrase that means ***"I am you, and you are me"*** or ***"You are my other me"*** or ***"I am another yourself."***

It reflects the interconnectedness and interdependence of all beings.

The notion of *In Lak'ech* vehemently states that we are all part of a larger whole and that our actions and behaviours have an impact on others. It is an understanding of a sense of unity amongst individuals. By honouring the inherent worth and value in others, we begin to appreciate and respect the interconnected web of life.

In Lak'ech serves as a reminder to have regard and care for another, to consider the well-being of others, and to act with kindness. It impels us to invest in harmonious relationships and have a sense of collective responsibility for the greater good.

While the origin of the *In Lak'ech* concept is attributed to the Mayan civilization, similar principles of interconnectedness and mutual respect can be found in various indigenous cultures across Mesoamerica. These teachings only underscore why the ties of relationships within communities and beyond are invaluable. And no meaningful relationships can have deep roots without the soil of compassion.

We will now examine the inseparable bond between compassion and deep coaching relationships. As we look into this dynamic connection, we will see the contrasts it holds within the conventional norms of coaching.

What are the Conventional Coaching Paradigms?

1. **Goal-oriented Coaching**: Traditional coaching often weighs heavily towards setting and achieving specific goals. Coaches work with clients to define objectives, create action plans, and track progress towards desired outcomes.

2. **Solution-focused Coaching**: This approach centres on finding solutions to specific challenges or problems. Coaches help clients unearth options, identify obstacles and develop strategies to beat them.

3. **Performance Improvement Coaching**: This is centred around boosting professional performance. Coaches work with clients to ascertain areas for improvement, develop skills and reach higher levels of success in their careers.

4. **Skills-based Coaching**: Coaches support clients in developing specific skills or competencies. They provide feedback, and practice opportunities to strengthen capabilities in desired areas, such as communication, leadership or time management.

What is it to Adopt a Daring Path Towards Transformation?

1. **Evoking Inner Evolution**: Unlike placing sole attention on external objectives, transformational coaching serves as a catalyst for fundamental human revolution. Coaches assist the clients in knowing their patterns and tendencies allowing them to pinpoint areas that need shifts. Partnering with the coach helps clarify one's intention and purpose for seeking inner change that further imparts direction and impetus for the journey.

2. **Inner Work and Self-reflection**: This approach zooms in on introspection and self-awareness. By addressing underlying emotional and psychological patterns, clients no longer feel controlled by past traumas or conditioned responses and can actively shape their future. They become more adept at recognizing triggers and responding in a balanced manner, thus reducing emotional reactivity.

3. **Embodied Coaching**: This approach recognizes the mind-body connection and explores the somatic experience of clients. Coaches help clients access their body's wisdom, integrating physical sensations, emotions and intuition into the coaching process.

4. **Narrative Coaching**: Coaches engage clients in storytelling and reframing their personal narratives. By reshaping the stories clients tell themselves individuals can change their interpretation of events, experiences and people. Ultimately, this process can lead to a sense of agency in shaping one's life.

Taking these bold paths expands coaching beyond goals to encompass so much more.

Here are concrete exercises for each of the above:

1. **Evoking Inner Evolution:**

    *   **Core Values Exploration:** Ask clients to identify their top five core values and reflect on how aligned they are with their current

life choices. Discuss any gaps and the probable ways to interweave these values more fully into their lives.

2. **Inner Work and Self-reflection**:

   ♦ **Belief Exploration**: Ask clients to identify a limiting belief that holds them back and contest its validity. Guide them in reframing the belief into a more empowering and supportive perspective.

3. **Embodied Coaching**:

   ♦ **Movement and Expression**: Guide clients in trying out expressive movement practices, such as dance, yoga, martial arts or such. Ask them to notice how their body responds and communicates during these activities.

4. **Narrative Coaching**:

   Rewriting Personal Stories: Ask clients to write down a specific life experience or roadblock they are facing. Encourage them to write a new narrative that rouses and uplifts them.

   ♦ **Future Self Journaling**: Prompt clients to imagine themselves five years in the future, living their ideal life. Ask them to journal about this future self, and describe their accomplishments, values and the steps that they took to get there.

These exercises provide practical ways to implement the concepts of transformational coaching.

Some more approaches that can be merged cohesively with novel approaches for deepening the client-coach relationship:

1. **Co-creation of Goals**: Research shows that engaging clients in the goal-setting process leads to higher levels of motivation and commitment.[84] A study conducted [referenced earlier too] by Grant et al. (2009) found that when individuals have a sense of autonomy and ownership over their goals, they are more likely to take proactive steps towards achieving them.[85]

2. **Strengths-based Approach**: Numerous studies have established the effectiveness of a strengths-based approach in coaching. Research by Linley, Nielsen, Gillett and Biswas-Diener (2010) showed that drawing attention to strengths improves well-being, satisfaction and performance.[86]

3. **Experiential Exercises**: Incorporating experiential exercises can reinforce the client's learning and emotional connection to the coaching process. For example, research conducted by Kearsley and Schneider (2013) evidenced that experiential activities, such as role-playing or simulations, make possible a better grasp and application of new skills.[87]

4. **Appreciative Inquiry**: Research conducted by Cooperrider, Whitney and Stavros (2008) has highlighted the benefits of appreciative inquiry in coaching. It is about amplifying the positive aspects of clients' experiences and aspirations like their past successes and envisioning a positive future, which creates a foundation of optimism and possibility.[88]

5. **Intuitive Coaching**: Develop the ability to tap into intuition and use it as a valuable tool in the coaching process. By trusting their intuition, coaches can unravel a lot.

6. **Accountability Structures**: Establish clear expectations, outline specific goals and regularly check in with clients to maintain accountability. This ensures that clients stay firm and committed to taking action towards their desired outcomes.

These techniques sometimes go beyond traditional strategies and offer unique avenues for connection, trust and personal development deepening the client-coach relationship.

A closing concept from tribal cultures that spotlights the importance of relationship ties is that of *Inipi* or the *sweat lodge ceremony*.

The ceremony is practised by Native American tribes, particularly the Lakota Sioux. It is a ritualistic and communal experience that involves a purification process through sweat and steam inside a ceremonial structure.

In the ceremony, individuals gather together in a small, dome-shaped lodge made of natural materials. The lodge represents the womb of Mother Earth, and the ceremony symbolizes rebirth and spiritual renewal. The intense heat and darkness inside the lodge create a testing environment that impels participants to support and rely on each other.

During the ceremony, participants talk about their prayers, stories and personal experiences. The deep level of sharing and vulnerability creates a strong bond among the participants, which promotes a sense of unity and interconnectedness. Through the ceremony, tribal communities highlight why relationships are instrumental, acknowledging that the collective strength and help of the community is a prerequisite for individual advancement.

Inipi or the sweat lodge ceremony serves as a reminder for honouring relationship ties and how shared experiences can create powerful connections and cement the bonds between individuals benefitting all.

If you truly loved yourself,
You could never hurt another.

– Buddha

Chapter 14
The Coaching Craft

In Chapter 14, we arrive at more nuanced coaching approaches, such as working with compassion-centric coaching practices and interlacing Buddhist principles into specific coaching methodologies.

A Zen Story, Which Reveals the True Nature of Enlightened Human Beings:

Two monks were cleaning their bowls by the river when they saw a scorpion struggling in the water. Without hesitation, one monk rescued it and got stung in the process.

As he returned to washing his bowl, he witnessed the scorpion slipping back into the water. Once again, he saved it, enduring another sting.

Curious, the second monk inquired, "Why do you keep saving the scorpion when you know its nature is to sting?"

The first monk replied with a smile, "Because it is my nature to save."

Practicing compassion is not easy, but definitely possible. It's in our nature.

Let us learn three specific approaches—*Tonglen*, *Naikan*-based Compassion Training—NBCT, and Sustainable Compassion Training.

1. *Tonglen* is a Tibetan Buddhist practice that questions the conventional approach of avoiding or pushing away suffering. Instead, it involves directly engaging with suffering. It helps to expand our capacity to be present with pain and respond to it with love and kindness.

   While empirical research specifically on *Tonglen* is limited, studies on related practices, such as loving-kindness meditation and compassion-focused interventions have shown various benefits. These include increased positive emotions, better social connections, and greater emotional resilience.[89]

By engaging in *Tonglen*, clients can co-relate to others' experiences, grow to be more compassionate and foster a greater sense of interconnectedness.

2. ***Naikan*-based NBCT**: *Naikan* is a Japanese method of self-reflection that encourages individuals to deeply examine their relationships and interactions with others. *Naikan*-based NBCT (*Naikan*-based narrative behaviour change technique) combines *Naikan* with narrative therapy and cognitive-behavioural techniques. It brings to the fore patterns of thoughts, emotions, and behaviours through structured self-reflection exercises that focus on relationships, gratitude and personal responsibility.[90]

3. **Sustainable Compassion Training (SCT)** is a programme developed by psychologists Thupten Jinpa and Paul Gilbert, which mingles elements of Tibetan Buddhism, evolutionary science and neuroscience, psychology, and other religious traditions to develop sustainable compassion. Derived from the practice traditions of Nyingma, Kagyu, and Geluk within Tibetan Buddhism, SCT has been adapted and informed by ongoing dialogue with psychological science.[91]

Research studies have verified the effectiveness of SCT. A study conducted by Jazaieri et al. (2018) found that participants who underwent SCT training showed major increases in self-compassion, compassion for others, and overall well-being compared to a control group. The training also led to reductions in depressive symptoms and anxiety, which indicates the potential therapeutic benefits of SCT.[92]

Furthermore, studies have shown the positive impact of SCT on neural mechanisms related to empathy and compassion. Krygier et al. (2013) used functional magnetic resonance imaging (fMRI) to investigate the neural effects of SCT practice.[93] They found that individuals who engaged in SCT training exhibited increased neural activation in brain regions which are associated with empathy and compassion and suggest that SCT can induce neuroplastic changes supporting prosocial emotions.

The adaptability of SCT across religious and cultural contexts is another noteworthy aspect. While rooted in Buddhism, SCT's teachings and practices have been carefully examined and adapted to make them accessible and relevant to individuals from diverse backgrounds. This inclusivity allows people of different faiths or no religious affiliation to benefit from SCT and its transformative effects.

Moreover, SCT underlines the importance of self-care and avoiding burnout among caregivers and helping professionals. Through self-regulation practices, SCT helps individuals prevent compassion fatigue, and maintain their wellness while extending compassion to others.

Overall, Sustainable Compassion Training is a robust and evidence-based approach that combines ancient wisdom and contemporary psychological insights.

In addition to SCT, two other notable approaches within the realm of compassion-focused coaching are cognitive-based compassion training (CBCT) and compassion cultivation training (CCT).

4. **Cognitive-Based Compassion Training (CBCT)**: It is a secular programme that blends elements of Tibetan Buddhist meditation practices with contemporary cognitive-behavioural techniques. Developed by Lobsang Tenzin Negi, CBCT aims to increase altruistic behaviour not surprisingly through intentional mindfulness and compassion for self and others. It draws upon the ancient wisdom of *lojong*, a practice within Indo-Tibetan Buddhism that purposes transforming one's mind. The training involves various meditation exercises, cognitive restructuring and perspective-taking practices.[94]

Research studies have shown promising results for CBCT in increasing compassion and reducing stress. For instance, a study conducted by Jazaieri et al. (2012) found that participants who underwent CBCT training were positively impacted.[95]

5. **Compassion Cultivation Training (CCT):** It is another evinced programme developed by Thupten Jinpa and colleagues at Stanford University's Centre for Compassion and Altruism Research and Education. CCT also draws from Tibetan Buddhist practices, psychology and contemplative neuroscience where participants through meditation practices, reflective exercises and group discussions experience the expression of compassion.

   Research on CCT has also confirmed its impact on various outcomes. A study conducted by Jazaieri et al. (2014) found that participants who completed CCT training showed sizeable upgrades in compassion-related variables compared to a waitlist control group.[96]

The use of CEB, CBCT, and CCT can contribute to the overall effectiveness of coaching interventions in personal and professional domains.[97]

A pertinent question to ask at this juncture is whether compassion can be acquired or cultivated.

Yes, it can be cultivated. The good news is that it is a learnable skill!

Fortunately, the development of compassion does not necessitate a prolonged commitment and can progress rapidly. Fascinatingly, a concise intervention lasting only seven minutes was discovered by Mantelou and Karakasidou (2017) to improve feelings of closeness, amplify compassion, and boost life satisfaction compared to individuals who did not receive compassion training.[98]

The prime point in compassion-based training is compassionate social mentality—a strong and wilful desire towards a compassionate self and a broader compassionate perspective (Gilbert, 2009).[99]

The efficacy of compassion-based training lies in its activation of the affiliative processing systems in the brain. Notably, it engages the myelinated parasympathetic nervous system, which governs our fight/flight response regulation.

Activation of the parasympathetic system when faced with perceived threats intuits safety and security, thus facilitating mentalization—a crucial ability to comprehend our mental state (Klimecki, Leiberg, Ricard and Singer, 2014).[100] This is responsible for the experience of sympathy, empathy and compassion.

Compassion training programmes have garnered well-deserved attention in the scientific and clinical communities due to their potential to cultivate and regulate compassion. Kirby (2017) identifies six empirically supported interventions that specifically intend to do so.[101] These interventions have already been discussed extensively in the previous chapters:

1. Loving-kindness meditation (LKM)

2. Compassion meditation

3. Compassion cultivation training (CCT)

4. Cognitive-based compassion training (CBCT)

5. Mindfulness-based compassionate living (MBCL)

6. Self-compassion training (SCT)

Furthermore, there are three very amazing *orientations of compassion*, described in Buddhist teachings:

1. Compassion for oneself (***Ninjō***, 自情): This orientation involves extending compassion and kindness towards oneself, recognizing one's suffering, and nurturing self-care.

2. Compassion for others (***Tanin***, 他人): This orientation involves extending compassion towards others, recognizing their suffering and wishing to alleviate it. An example of this orientation is engaging in acts of service towards others, volunteering for a charitable cause or offering support to someone in need.

3. Compassion without distinction (**Banbetsu**, 万別): This orientation goes beyond individual boundaries and extends compassion to all living beings without discrimination. It involves recognizing the interconnectedness of all beings and feeling a sense of universal compassion.

These three orientations work together to encompass oneself, others and all beings in a compassionate embrace.

The pursuant question is:

Is compassion quantifiable? Measurable?

Yes, compassion can be measured using various scales, which are developed over the years by researchers in the field. These compassion scales are designed to assess an individual's level of compassion or his tendency to experience and express compassion towards others. Here are a few examples of compassion scales:

1. **Compassionate Love Scale** (CLS): Developed by Sprecher and Fehr (2005) this scale measures the disposition of compassionate love, which refers to feelings of care, kindness and concern for others. It also assesses the emotional, cognitive and behavioural aspects of compassionate love.[102]

2. **Self-compassion Scale (SCS):** The SCS gauges an individual's level of self-compassion, which involves being kind, understanding and forgiving towards oneself during difficult times. It assesses different facets, such as self-kindness and common humanity.

3. **Interpersonal Reactivity Index** (IRI): Although not exclusively focused on compassion, the IRI includes a subscale called *empathic concern* that assesses an individual's ability to experience concern for others in distress. It measures the emotional and cognitive aspects of compassion.

These compassion scales provide researchers and practitioners with tools to estimate different dimensions of compassion in individuals. By measuring compassion, researchers can study its effects, assay its relationship with various outcomes and evaluate the efficacy of interventions.

In the context of coaching, using compassion scales in coaching can provide a baseline assessment of a client's compassion, which can inform the coaching process. By administering compassion scales at the beginning of coaching engagements and periodically throughout the process, coaches can gain insights into their clients' compassion-related strengths and areas for growth.

Coaches can determine definite areas where clients may need backing in developing their compassion skills. Additionally, compassion scales can also help evaluate the effectiveness of these customized coaching interventions.

It is important to note that compassion scales should be used as one component of a comprehensive coaching approach. They provide valuable data, but they should be complemented with other coaching techniques, such as active listening, powerful questioning and experiential exercises to enable a holistic experience.

Compassion scales typically include a series of statements or items that individuals respond to, based on their experiences and feelings. The specific statements can vary depending on the scale being used but here are some examples of the types of statements that may be included:

1. **Empathy**: "I often feel deeply moved by other people's emotions."

2. **Kindness**: "I do my best to help others in need."

3. **Non-judgemental**: "I try to understand others without criticizing or judging them."

4. **Caring for others**: "I genuinely care about the well-being of others."

5. **Self-compassion**: "I am understanding and kind towards myself when I'm struggling."

6. **Forgiveness**: "I am able to forgive others for their mistakes or wrongdoings."

7. **Altruism**: "I willingly forgo my interests to help others in dire need."

8. **Emotional warmth**: "I feel a sense of warmth and affection towards others."

Participants typically respond to these statements using a rating scale, such as a **Likert scale**, to indicate the extent to which they agree or disagree with each statement. The responses are then used to calculate scores that reflect the individual's level of compassion.

These statements are designed to capture the thoughts, feelings and behaviours associated with compassion, and allow individuals to self-assess and discern their compassionate tendencies.

Love and compassion are necessities, not luxuries. Without them, humanity cannot survive.

– Dalai Lama XIV, *The Art of Happiness.*

Conclusion:

Chapter 14 expanded our coaching horizons and we discovered new tools to empower our coaching relationships and support clients.

The chapter underscored an important fact: compassion is not just an innate trait but a skill that can be learned and nurtured. This revelation opens up new vistas for coaching, as it suggests that individuals can indeed amplify their capacity for compassion.

Additionally, we tackled the question of whether compassion can be quantified, and the answer is affirmative. Researchers have developed compassion scales, providing a means to measure an individual's compassion level and their propensity to extend compassion to others.

This chapter reaffirmed the synergy between Buddhism, compassion, and coaching, illustrating how they enrich our coaching repertoire and nurture personal and collective growth.

As we wrap up this chapter, we carry with us the knowledge that compassion is not a static quality but a dynamic force that can be harnessed and refined through dedicated practice. It is a skill that holds the power to transform coaching relationships.

Sometimes it's better to be kind than to be right. We do not need an intelligent mind that speaks, but a patient heart that listens.

– Buddha

Chapter 15
Buddha 2.0

Introduction

Step into the 21st century and witness the role shift of Buddha, the timeless sage, as he dons a modern guise as the exemplification of coaching wisdom. Amidst this age of swift and constant change, Buddha's teachings echo through the works of contemporary thinkers. By drawing captivating analogies between Buddha's ancient sagacity and the fresh perspectives of modern thought leaders, we unearth the hidden gems of his teachings and present lessons for Gen Z, industry leaders and the entire coach community.

A Zen Story:

During a tumultuous time in Korea, a rebel army descended upon a peaceful town, causing panic among the monks of a Zen temple. They scattered, seeking safety, but the abbot stood unwavering.

As the dust settled, the imposing figure of the army's general filled the temple. He expected reverence and submission, and his voice thundered as he declared, 'Don't you know that you are looking at a man who can run you through without blinking?'

'And you,' replied the abbot strongly, 'are looking at a man who can be run through without blinking.'

In the midst of this tension, the abbot's response was resolute.

In that charged moment, their eyes locked. The general, accustomed to domination, saw something different in the abbot's unwavering gaze—a reflection of inner strength, unyielding in the face of adversity. Without further words, the general bowed in recognition and withdrew.

This Zen parable reminds us that true strength lies not in domination but in inner peace and resilience, qualities that can inspire awe even in the most challenging of circumstances.

This Zen story can be related to the qualities of Buddha vis-à-vis a modern coach, drawing parallels between the abbot's wisdom and the attributes of an effective coach:

1. **Emotional Resilience**: Much like the abbot, a modern coach needs emotional resilience. They must remain composed and not be easily swayed by external pressures or emotions. In coaching, this resilience allows them to create a safe and supportive space for their clients, even in puzzling situations.

2. **True Nature**: The abbot's understanding of his true nature symbolizes a coach's deep self-awareness. A modern coach must be in touch with their own values, beliefs, and biases to effectively guide their clients without imposing their views.

3. **Questioning and Humility**: The abbot's inner attitude of questioning and humility aligns with a coach's role as a curious and non-judgemental listener. Modern coaches ask thought-provoking questions to help clients explore their beliefs, thoughts, and behaviours. They approach coaching with an open mind and a willingness to learn from their clients.

4. **Problem-Solving**: Just as the abbot's response to the general's threat reflected his degree of realization, a modern coach's ability to help clients deal with predicaments showcases their coaching proficiency. They support clients in finding their own solutions and take action toward their goals.

5. **Standing for Truth and Justice**: The abbot's willingness to stand his ground for truth and justice resonates with a modern coach's commitment to ethical coaching practices. They prioritize the

well-being of their clients, ensure confidentiality, and uphold ethical standards in the coaching relationship.

Essentially, this Zen story depicts the core attributes of an effective coach. These attributes, closely aligned with those of the abbot in the story and featuring the essence of Buddha's teachings, are indispensable for modern coaches. By personifying these qualities, coaches can empower their clients on the path to success and personal growth.

Buddha—The Modern *Father of Coaching*

1. Buddha as *The Father of Coaching* in the 21st Century:

If Buddha was alive today, he would undoubtedly be celebrated as *The Father of Coaching*, as his doctrines stand for the core principles and practices that underpin the coaching field. Modern thinkers like Eckhart Tolle and Brené Brown, influential in their own right, are in essence the reflections of Buddha's wisdom and depth.

For instance, Tolle's work on presence and mindfulness aligns with the heart of Buddha's teachings on being fully present in the moment. Brown's rich body of effort in the area of vulnerability echoes Buddha's teachings on not forsaking impermanence but choosing to relinquish attachment. In coaching, Buddha's style would nevertheless reverberate with the coming together of mindfulness, self-reflection and compassionate guidance to bring about enabling shifts.[103]

2. Buddha as a True Coach in His Time:

During his time, Buddha could be said to have displayed all the qualities of an exemplary coach. While actively listening, he assisted the disciples to inquire into the nature of their suffering and find liberation from it. Buddha's persona was replete with qualities that resonate with the principles of coaching today and this alignment provides a compelling case for the empowering nature of his approach.[104]

As with many historical or spiritual figures, there will be speculation and interpretation involved in understanding how Buddha's coaching-like qualities align with modern coaching. While we can draw parallels and identify similarities, it is crucial to recognize that the historical context and cultural norms of ancient India were different from contemporary coaching practices. Yet, we stand to benefit from them immensely.

3. Buddha's Enduring Relevance and Lessons for Gen Z:

The hyperconnected, digitally driven society poses unique challenges to this generation. Despite living over 2,500 years ago, Buddha's teachings are extraordinarily pertinent and offer valuable lessons for Gen Z.

Mindfulness in the Digital Age: The prevalence of digital devices and constant connectivity can lead to information overload and distractions. Benefitting from mindfulness and being fully present in the moment, Gen Z can regain focus, reduce anxiety and develop healthier relationships with technology.

Overcoming Comparison Culture: Social media can fuel a culture of comparison, which leads to feelings of inadequacy and self-doubt. Buddha's teachings on self-compassion prod Gen Z to find value in their unique journey, and credit authenticity, rather than craving validation from external sources.

Coping with Stress and Anxiety: The fast-paced and competitive nature of modern life can contribute to heightened stress levels for Gen Z. Buddha's teachings on non-attachment offer tools to combat tension and traumas and allow a sense of calm to descend.

Life is full of challenges and uncertainties. Clinging tightly to outcomes, possessions, or expectations is like trying to hold onto a rushing river, which only creates stress and anxiety.

Buddha's wisdom encourages us to release this tight grip. Through non-attachment, we gain the ability to deal with life's currents calmly. This practice promotes flexibility, reduces the impact of setbacks, and boosts resilience in stressful situations.

Non-attachment doesn't mean disengagement from life; instead, it fosters a deep and peaceful engagement. It frees us from excessive worry about the future or dwelling on the past. This shift in mindset can bring serenity amidst life's chaos and aid in managing stress and anxiety, particularly for Gen Z.

Empathy and Connection: In a digital world, real human connection can sometimes be overlooked. Buddha's teachings on compassion gently nudge Gen Z to build genuine relationships, find meaning in a sense of community and value inclusivity and support for one another.

Pursuit of Purpose and Meaning: Gen Z today hunts for purpose and meaning in their lives beyond material success. Buddha's teachings on finding one's true path and inner fulfilment can guide them in discovering their passions and aligning their actions with their values.

Learnings on Non-attachment: They can help combat the materialistic and consumer-driven culture, as well as develop an appreciation for the present moment and authentic connections.

Here non-attachment urges us to let go of the constant desire for more. This shift in perspective can help us break free from the cycle of constantly seeking external sources of happiness and find contentment within ourselves and our relationships.

These teachings, found in ***the Dhammapada*** and other Buddhist texts, can empower Gen Z to lead lives with resoluteness and make positive contributions to society.[105]

Let us read some quotes that highlight how Buddha's teachings align with practices found in today's coaching profession:

Present-Moment Awareness: Focus on *the here and now*! This aligns with the idea of appreciating the present rather than dwelling on the past or worrying about the future. As Buddha said, "The secret of health for both mind and body is not to mourn for the past, not to worry about the future or not to anticipate troubles but to live in the present moment wisely and earnestly."

Compassion: Buddha said, "If your compassion does not include yourself, it is incomplete." This quote reflects the emphasis on self-compassion and the recognition that self-care is an essential aspect of supporting others.

Non-judgement and Acceptance: Buddha said, "You can search throughout the entire universe for someone more deserving of your love and affection than you are yourself, and that person is not to be found anywhere. You yourself, as much as anybody in the entire universe, deserve your love and affection." This quote on self-acceptance reiterates what is often missed.

Questioning and Inquiry: Buddha said, "Believe nothing, no matter where you read it or who has said it, not even if I have said it unless it agrees with your reason and common sense." This quote highlights the coach's role in facilitating clients' independent thinking and self-discovery.

Personal Growth and Development: Buddha said, "The mind is everything. What you think, you become." Here we find that mindset, thoughts, and beliefs hold great power in shaping one's reality.

Further, let us see how the Buddha's doctrines and theories of contemporary thinkers would come together beautifully:

Parable of the Raft:

The parable of the raft [shared earlier], illustrates the impermanence of teachings, and contemporary thinkers, such as Alan Watts too, reinforce the idea of letting go of rigid concepts. Watts says not to cling to any particular belief system but rather, to use the related teachings as a means to awaken our innate wisdom and discover our true nature (Watts, 1951).[106]

The Buddha on Suffering:

The Buddha's teaching on suffering caused by both physical pain and the mental reactions to it and the insights of Viktor Frankl are in line. Frankl, a renowned existential psychologist, states that while we may not have control over external circumstances, we can choose our response to them, thus freeing ourselves from unnecessary suffering (Frankl, 1946).[107]

The Parable of the Mustard Seed:

The parable of the mustard seed [shared earlier], in which the Buddha espouses the universality of suffering, relates with the views of contemporary mindfulness advocate, Jon Kabat-Zinn. Kabat-Zinn highlights the power of mindfulness in recognizing and embracing our suffering, which leads to healing and transformation (Kabat-Zinn, 2005).[108]

Conclusion:

By intertwining traditional parables with the work of modern thought leaders, we begin to appreciate that the Buddha's words stand true even millennia later. It is through this harmonious blending that Buddha 2.0 emerges as a beacon of guidance, thus bridging the wisdom of the past with the transformative potential of the present.

We are what we think. All that we are arises with our thoughts.
With our thoughts, we make the world.

– Buddha

Chapter 16
Buddha and AI

In this chapter, the teachings of the Buddha and the field of artificial intelligence (AI) present interesting facets and dimensions to explore. While the nucleus of Buddha's teachings is the human mind, consciousness and spiritual growth, AI is centred around developing intelligent machines that can perform tasks that traditionally required human intelligence. These seemingly disparate domains warrant a discussion on the nature of consciousness, the limits of artificial intelligence and the ethical implications of creating intelligent beings.

The examination of these dimensions can help us understand both human cognition and the potential of AI and allow us sneak peeks into the nature of existence and the future of intelligent technologies.

A Buddhist Parable:

Two Buddhist monks arrived at a riverbank. They encountered a flooded river, and a woman stood there in distress, seeking help to cross. She explained that her children were alone and hungry on the other side. One of the monks declined to assist, while the other kindly lifted the woman onto his back and carried her across the river.

After safely reaching the other side, the first monk expressed his shock and disapproval, as monks typically avoid physical contact with women. He was troubled by his companion's actions.

The second monk responded, "Do you mean you're still carrying the woman in your thoughts? I let her go at the riverbank long ago."

The story of the two monks encountering a woman by the river beautifully illustrates the intricate interplay between compassion, practicality, and ethics, which holds significant relevance in the realms of coaching and AI.

The monk who helped the woman demonstrated compassion and a pragmatic approach to a situation, prioritizing immediate human needs over rigid rules. However, the initial hesitation of the other monk reflects the ethical concerns associated with their roles as monks and the potential transgression of their vows.

In the context of coaching and AI, this story underscores that ethical considerations are of paramount importance. Ethical principles should serve as the unwavering foundation upon which decisions and actions are based. And keeping compassion and practicality aligned with a robust ethical framework is of prime importance to ensure the well-being of individuals.

Just as the second monk left the woman behind on the riverbank after fulfilling a humanitarian need, ethical frameworks should remain steadfast in guiding the development and application of AI and coaching practices. This steadfast commitment to ethics ensures that compassionate actions are always undertaken with the utmost respect for ethical conduct, fostering a harmonious balance between human welfare, practicality, and unwavering ethical principles.

Let's delve into how the fusion of Buddhist principles and AI ethics can shape a future that upholds human values while integrating artificial intelligence seamlessly:

1. **Ethical AI:** As AI increasingly commingles into various aspects of society, ethical considerations arise. Adopting Buddhist principles of compassion and non-harm can help guide the development and deployment of AI technologies in ways that align with human values and safeguard well-being. Coaches and AI developers need to ensure privacy, data security, and transparency in the use of AI technologies. Coaches using AI-powered tools should ensure informed consent from clients regarding data collection, storage and usage by respecting their privacy and confidentiality as guided by the International Coaching Federation (ICF) in the ICF Code of Ethics. Finally, the human element of coaching, such as empathy, intuition and the ability to build trust, remains essential and cannot be fully replaced by AI.

2. **Artificial General Intelligence (AGI) and Enlightenment**: The Buddha's quest for enlightenment and liberation from suffering can be seen as a metaphorical pursuit of a higher level of consciousness. The concept of AGI, a hypothetical form of AI that possesses general cognitive abilities, is comparable to humans in which a machine can learn and think like a human. For this to be possible, AGI would need self-awareness and consciousness, so it could solve problems, adapt to its surroundings and perform a broader range of tasks. It however raises philosophical questions. Therefore, closely analysing the confluence of AGI and Buddhism could shed light on the nature of human consciousness and the possibilities for AI to reach higher levels of understanding.

3. **Human-AI Collaboration**: Interconnectedness and interdependence are integral to Buddhism. Rather than viewing AI as a replacement for human intelligence, a complementary perspective can be adopted, which relies on a coalition between humans and AI. By leveraging AI's computational power and analytical capabilities, combined with human creativity, wisdom and intuition, we can address complex challenges and enhance decision-making processes.

The amalgam of the Buddha's teachings and AI should be approached with thoughtfulness, ethical deliberations and a correct understanding of the limitations, as well as the potential impact of AI on individuals and society.

The Buddha's teachings, coaching and AI crisscross, thus posing intriguing possibilities for individual development and profound life-changing encounters.

Let's explore how these seemingly divergent worlds can come together to create a more accessible, effective, and ethical coaching environment:

- **Mindfulness and Self-awareness**: AI-powered tools, such as meditation apps or wearable devices, can support individuals [coachees] in developing mindfulness and tracking their progress, thus supporting in building their self-awareness in real time.

Example: Mindfulness meditation apps, such as **Headspace** or **Calm** leverage AI algorithms to provide personalized meditation programmes, which are tailored to individuals' needs and preferences.[109]

- **Personalized Coaching Experiences:** AI technologies, such as chatbots or virtual coaches, are no more fiction and can deliver personalized coaching experiences. By poring over data from various sources, such as assessments, feedback and user interactions, AI systems can generate customized recommendations, and amplify the effectiveness of coaching interventions while ensuring that the ethical principles aren't compromised.

  Example: AI-powered virtual coaching platforms, such as **CoachHub**, utilize natural language processing and machine learning to analyse user input and deliver customized service.[110]

- **Enhanced Access to Coaching Resources**: AI can democratize access to coaching resources by providing online platforms, virtual communities and self-guided tools. Through AI-powered platforms, coaching content, educational materials and peer support become available to all, which allows individuals to engage in self-directed learning at their pace and convenience.

  Example: Online coaching platforms, such as **BetterUp** make effective use of AI algorithms to match individuals with suitable coaches, based on their goals, preferences and personality traits.[111]

- **Data-driven Insights and Feedback:** By perceiving patterns, trends, and correlations in large datasets, AI algorithms can uncover areas for improvement, and track progress over time. This information can inform coaching strategies and facilitate goal setting, thus making the coaching process an effectual one.

  Example: AI-powered sentiment analysis tools, such as IBM Watson, can analyse coaching session transcripts to provide coaches with intuitive understanding of clients' emotional states and progress.[112]

AI technologies can contribute to the accessibility and effectiveness of coaching, but it is essential to balance their benefits with the human connection and Buddhist wisdom to encash upon a myriad of opportunities and defy challenges while staying ethical.

Conclusion:

To summarize, the juxtaposition of Buddha's body of teachings and artificial intelligence in this chapter has unveiled thought-provoking insights. We've explored the realms of human consciousness, the potential of AI, and the ethical considerations that accompany its development. These reflections provide valuable glimpses into the nature of existence and the trajectory of intelligent technology, stimulating contemplation about our ethical responsibilities in shaping a mindful and tech-infused future.

If you do not change direction,
you may end up where you are heading.

– Buddha

Epilogue: The Journey Continues

My dear fellow readers, in this epilogue, we summarily reflect on the path that we undertook in *Coaching Compassion & Leadership*. We acknowledge that the learnings and doings of compassionate coaching is an ongoing process, which support us in *being* a compassionate coach—both in our professional practice and in our lives.

Throughout the book, we have pondered the dynamic planes of compassionate coaching and recorded its reverberance with modernity and relevance. We now take a fresh look at the *eightfold path* of compassionate coaching. Let me distil it for you:

1. **Authentic Perception:** This is the key to unlocking the mysteries of our clients' hearts! Receive and honour their unique stories and dreams, for therein lies the spark of compelling change.

2. **Heartfelt Intentions:** As coaches, our mission is to work from a ground fertile with compassion, kindness and wisdom. Provide a haven for your clients, where judgement dare not tread.

3. **Rousing Communication:** Words are your magic wand, dear coaches! Use them with authenticity, empathy, and simplicity to catalyse newfound self-awareness and growth in clients.

4. **Ethical Alchemy:** Integrity is your crown jewel, my friends! Uphold confidentiality and regard your clients' well-being as foremost, for trust is the cornerstone of your sacred bond.

5. **Purposeful Alignment:** Let your values guide you like the North Star, as you lead your clients towards purposeful shifts and meaningful bearing.

6. **Unwavering Dedication**: The pursuit of greatness demands lifelong learning and unyielding dedication. Stay hungry, stay curious and let your insatiable thirst for growth fuel your coaching brilliance.

7. **Mindful Presence**: In the chaos of this relentless world, call for stillness and present-moment awareness. Fully attune yourself to your clients' narratives and emotions, and watch the magic unfold.

8. **Focused Brilliance**: Amidst the cacophony of distractions, let your concentration be your secret weapon. Your undivided attention will pave the way for breakthroughs and best realizations.

Remember, compassionate coaching is a living, breathing practice that knows no bounds. As you step beyond these pages, let every coaching session become an invitation to change lives and hearts, and may it ripple outward to create a more harmonious and compassionate world for generations to come.

The legacy we create is one of hope—echoing through the passages of time. Through the dance of compassionate coaching let us continue to inspire, uplift, and infuse our work with meaning. The world awaits our transformative power. Onward, my fellow coaches, for the journey continues!

Appendix

Here are some resources that can provide insights into the concept of intuition:

1. ***Blink: The Power of Thinking Without Thinking*** by Malcolm Gladwell: This book explores the power of intuition and rapid decision-making based on unconscious thinking processes.

2. ***The Intuitive Way: The Definitive Guide to Increasing Your Awareness*** by Penney Peirce: This book offers practical techniques and exercises to develop and trust your intuition.

3. ***The Power of Intuition: How to Use Your Gut Feelings to Make Better Decisions at Work*** by Gary Klein: The author explores the role of intuition in decision-making by drawing from his research in cognitive psychology.

4. ***Intuition: Knowing Beyond Logic*** by Osho: In this book, Osho delves into the nature of intuition, as well as offers insights and practices to cultivate and harness its power.

5. ***The Gift of Intuition: Guidance on Love, Career and Relationships from Extraordinary People*** by Kaya and Christiane Muller: This book features interviews with renowned individuals who rely on their intuition in various aspects of life.

6. ***The Art of Intuition: Cultivating Your Inner Wisdom*** by Sophy Burnham: The author explores the nature of intuition, provides guidance on developing intuitive abilities and shares inspiring stories of individuals who have embraced their intuitive gifts.

These resources offer diverse perspectives and practical techniques for understanding and developing intuition. Exploring these works can deepen your understanding and provide practical tools to tap into your intuitive wisdom.

References

1. Lama, P. G. (1997). *Fire Under the Snow: True Story of a Tibetan Monk.* Penguin Books.

2. a) Analayo. (2003). *Compassion and Emptiness in Early Buddhist Meditation.* Windhorse Publications.

   b) Bodhi, B. (2012). *The Numerical Discourses of the Buddha: A Translation of the Aṅguttara Nikāya.* Wisdom Publications.

   c) Dalai Lama. (2001). *The Compassionate Life.* Wisdom Publications.

   d) Harvey, P. (2013). *An Introduction to Buddhism: Teachings, History and Practices.* Cambridge University Press.

   e) Nyanaponika Thera. (1998). *The Heart of Buddhist Meditation: A Handbook of Mental Training Based on the Buddha's Way of Mindfulness.* Weiser Books.

3. Theeboom, T., Beersma, B., & van Vianen, A. E. M. (2013). *Does coaching work? A meta-analysis on the effects of coaching on individual level outcomes in an organizational context.* The Journal of Positive Psychology, Advance online publication. http://dx.doi.org/10.1080/17439760.2013.837499

4. Grant, A. M., Curtayne, L., & Burton, G. (2009). *Executive coaching enhances goal attainment, resilience and workplace well-being: A randomized controlled study.* The Journal of Positive Psychology, 4(4), 396-407.

5. Maxwell, A. (2009). *How do business coaches experience the boundary between coaching and therapy/counseling?* Coaching: An International Journal of Theory, Research and Practice, 2, 149-162. https://doi.org/10.1080/17521880902930311.

6. Fredrickson, B. L., Cohn, M. A., Coffey, K. A., Pek, J., & Finkel, S. M. (2008). *Open hearts build lives: Positive emotions, induced through*

loving-kindness meditation, build consequential personal resources. Journal of Personality and Social Psychology, 95(5), 1045–1062. https://doi.org/10.1037/a0013262

7. *Ksitigarbha Bodhisattva: The Vow to Liberate All Beings from Hell,* Buddhistdoor Global.

8. Gallwey, W. T. (1997). *The Inner Game of Tennis: The Classic Guide to the Mental Side of Peak Performance.* Random House Trade Paperbacks.

9. Hamilton, E. (2013). *Mythology. New York.* Back Bay Books.

    a) Plato. (2005). *The Dialogues of Plato.* Translated by Benjamin Jowett. Oxford University Press.

    b) Magill, F. N. (Ed.). (1998). *The Ancient World: Dictionary of World Biography.* Routledge.

10. Theoi Project. (n.d.). *Kentauros Kheiron.* Retrieved from https://www.theoi.com/Georgikos/KentaurosKheiron.html

11. a) Plato. (2005). *The Dialogues of Plato.* Translated by Benjamin Jowett. Oxford University Press.

    b) Magill, F. N. (Ed.). (1998). *The Ancient World: Dictionary of World Biography.* Routledge.

12. Greeka. (n.d.). *Orpheus and Eurydice - Greek Myths.* Retrieved from https://www.greeka.com/greece-myths/orpheus-eurydice/

13. Dalley, Stephanie (Translator). (2008). *Myths from Mesopotamia: Creation, the Flood, Gilgamesh and Others.* Oxford University Press.

14. Anonymous. (n.d.). *The Epic of Gilgamesh* (Tablet IX). Retrieved from https://www.ancienttexts.org/library/mesopotamian/gilgamesh/tab9.htm

15. Kramer, S. N. (1997). *Inanna: Queen of Heaven and Earth: Her Stories and Hymns from Sumer.* University of Texas Press.

16. a) McEwan, G. (2008). *The Incas – New Perspectives.* W. W. Norton & Company.

b) Jones, D. (2011). *World of the Ancient Incas: The Extraordinary History of the Hidden Civilizations of the First Peoples of the South American Andes, With over 200 Photographs and Illustrations.* Southwater.

c) Jones, D. *The Inca Empire: An Illustrated History.* Anness Publishing.

17. The Gita Society. (n.d.). *Read Bhagavad Gita.* The Gita Society. https://www.gita-society.com/Read-bhagavad-gita.html

18. International Coach Federation. (n.d.). *Code of Ethics.* Retrieved from https://coachingfederation.org/ethics/code-of-ethics

19. Grant, A. M., Curtayne, L., & Burton, G. (2009). *Executive coaching enhances goal attainment, resilience, and workplace well-being: A randomized controlled study. The Journal of Positive Psychology, 4*(5), 396–407.

20. a) Davidson, R. J., Kabat-Zinn, J., Schumacher, J., Rosenkranz, M., Muller, D., Santorelli, S. F., Sheridan, J. F., et al. (2003). *Alterations in Brain and Immune Function Produced by Mindfulness Meditation. Psychosomatic Medicine, 65,* 564-570. https://doi.org/10.1097/01.PSY.0000077505.67574.E3

b) Shapiro, S. L., Carlson, L. E., Astin, J. A., & Freedman, B. (2006). *Mechanisms of mindfulness. Journal of clinical psychology, 62*(3), 373-386.

21. a) Fletcher, K., Yang, Y., Johnson, S. L., Berk, M., Perich, T., Cotton, S., Jones, S., Lapsley, S., Michalak, E., & Murray, G. (2019). *Buffering against maladaptive perfectionism in bipolar disorder: The role of self-compassion. Journal of affective disorders, 250,* 132–139. https://doi.org/10.1016/j.jad.2019.03.003

b) Siegel, R. D., Germer, C. K., & Olendzki, A. (2009). *Mindfulness: What is it? Where did it come from? In F. Didonna (Ed.), Clinical handbook of mindfulness* (pp. 17–35). Springer Science + Business Media. https://doi.org/10.1007/978-0-387-09593-6_2

22. a) Bohlmeijer, E., Prenger, R., Taal, E., & Cuijpers, P. (2010). *The effects of mindfulness-based stress reduction therapy on mental health of adults with a chronic medical disease: A meta-analysis.* Journal of Psychosomatic Research, 68(6), 539–544. https://doi.org/10.1016/j.jpsychores.2009.10.005

   b) Fredrickson, B. L., Cohn, M. A., Coffey, K. A., Pek, J., & Finkel, S. M. (2008). *Open Hearts Build Lives: Positive Emotions, Induced Through Loving-Kindness Meditation, Build Consequential Personal Resources.* Journal of Personality and Social Psychology, 95(5), 1045–1062. https://doi.org/10.1037/a0013262

   c) Lyubomirsky, S., King, L., & Diener, E. (2005). *The Benefits of Frequent Positive Affect: Does Happiness Lead to Success?* Psychological Bulletin, 131(6), 803–855. DOI: 10.1037/0033-2909.131.6.803

23. a) Mandela, N. (1995). *Long Walk to Freedom.* Abacus.

   b) Sampson, A. (2000). *Mandela: The Authorized Biography.* Vintage.

   c) Mandela, N. (2011). *Conversations With Myself.* Picador.

24. Huang Po. (2007). *The Zen Teaching of Huang Po: The Classic Zen Text On the Transmission of Mind.* Grove Press.

25. Gilbert, P. (2010). *A New Approach to Life's Challenges.* New Harbinger Publications Inc.

26. Loori, J. D. (2002). *Art of Just Sitting: Essential Writings on the Zen Practice of Shikantaza.* Wisdom Publications.

27. Scharmer, C. O. (2009). *Theory U: Learning from the Future as It Emerges.* Berrett-Koehler Publishers.

28. Rosenberg, M. B. (1999). *Nonviolent Communication: A Language of Life.* Puddledancer Press.

29. Cooperrider, D. L., & Srivastva, S. (1987). *Appreciative Inquiry. Research in Organizational Change and Development, 1*(1), 129-169.

30. a) White, M., & Epston, D. (1990). *Narrative Means to Therapeutic Ends.* W. W. Norton & Company.

    b) Monk, G. (1996). *Narrative Therapy in Practice - The Archaeology of Hope.* Jossey-Bass Inc., U.S.

31. Radin, D. I., & Schlitz, M. J. (2005). *Gut feelings, intuition, and emotions: An exploratory study. Journal of Alternative & Complementary Medicine, 11*(1), 85-91.

32. *Dhamma Talks.* (n.d.). Sāmaññaphala Sutta: *The Fruits of the Contemplative Life* (MN 21). Retrieved from https://www.dhammatalks.org/suttas/MN/MN21.html

33. *Vipassana Meditation as taught by S.N. Goenka.* (n.d.). *Angulimala.* Retrieved from https://www.vridhamma.org/Angulimala#:~:text=Angulimala%20threw%20away%20his%20weapons,agreed%20to%20leave%20him%20alone.

34. The Amaravati Sangha. (2004). *Karaniya Metta Sutta: The Buddha's Words on Loving-Kindness (Sn 1.8 PTS: Sn 143-152). Translated from the Pali.*

35. Singer, T. (2013, June 24). *Feeling Others' Pain: Transforming Empathy into Compassion. Breakthroughs in Cognitive Neuroscience: Highlighting Influential Research from the Past 20 Years.*

36. Breines, J. G., & Chen, S. (2012). *Self-compassion increases self-improvement motivation. Personality & Social Psychology Bulletin, 38*(9), 1133–1143. https://doi.org/10.1177/0146167212445599

37. **Doidge, N. (n.d.).** *The Brain's Way of Healing: Remarkable Discoveries and Recoveries from the Frontiers of Neuroplasticity.* **Penguin Random House.**

38. Tomlin, A. M., & Viehweg, S. A. (2016). *Tackling the Tough Stuff: A Home Visitor's Guide to Supporting Families at Risk.* Brookes.

39. Bradley, C. (2018, August 15). *The Power of Pause: Discover how to up your game and perform your best.* Mindful. https://www.mindful.org/the-power-of-pause/

40. Google. (n.d.). *Project Aristotle: A case study in psychological safety.* Retrieved from Google internal documents.

41. Edmondson, A. C. (2018). *How to Build Psychological Safety for Learning & Innovation.* Wiley.

42. W. L. Gore & Associates. (n.d.). *The Gore Story.* Retrieved from https://www.gore.com/about/the-gore-story

43. Somers, M. (2021, November 1). *The 3 leadership types in a nimble organization.* MIT Sloan Ideas Made to Matter. Retrieved from https://mitsloan.mit.edu/ideas-made-to-matter/3-leadership-types-a-nimble-organization

44. McKinsey & Company. (2023). *The State of Organizations 2023.* Retrieved fromhttps://www.mckinsey.com/~/media/mckinsey/business%20functions/people%20and%20organizational%20performance/our%20insights/the%20state%20of%20organizations%202023/the-state-of-organizations-2023.pdf

45. Stone, K. (2022, December 2). The Impact Of Employee Engagement On Productivity. *Elevate, Engage, Share.* Gallup Reports.

46. *Haiilo. (n.d.). 12 Steps to a Successful Enterprise Agile Transformation. Haiilo Blog.* https://haiilo.com/blog/12-steps-to-a-successful-enterprise-agile-transformation/

47. *Edelman. (2021). 21st Annual Edelman Trust Barometer. Fieldwork conducted from October 19 to November 18, 2020.*

48. Duchek, S. (2020). *Organizational resilience: A capability-based conceptualization. Business Research, 13,* 215–246. https://doi.org/10.1007/s40685-019-0085-7

49. Hardy, A.-C. (2016, March 1). *Agile Team Organisation: Squads, Chapters, Tribes and Guilds*. Retrieved from https://achardypm.medium.com/agile-team-organisation-squads-chapters-tribes-and-guilds-80932ace0fdc

50. *Amazon Web Services. (n.d.). Introduction to DevOps on AWS: Two-Pizza Teams. Retrieved from* https://docs.aws.amazon.com/whitepapers/latest/introduction-devops-aws/two-pizza-teams.html

51. Thai, J. (n.d.). *Distributing Authority: The story behind Zappos's shift to Holacracy. Wavelength.* Retrieved from https://wavelength.asana.com/zappos-self-managed-team/#:~:text=Created%20by%20former%20programmer%20Brian,of%20becoming%20more%20city%2Dlike.

52. Gallup. (2023). *State of the Global Workplace: 2023* (Report 2023). Retrieved from https://www.gallup.com/workplace/349484/state-of-the-global-workplace.aspx

53. Michaelson, C., Pratt, M. G., Grant, A. M., & Dunn, C. P. (2014). *Meaningful Work: Connecting Business Ethics and Organization Studies. Journal of Business Ethics, 121*(1), 77–90. http://www.jstor.org/stable/42921366

54. a) Oswald, A., Proto, E., & Sgroi, D. (2009). *Happiness and Productivity.* Institute for the Study of Labor (IZA), IZA Discussion Papers, 1. https://doi.org/10.1086/681096

    b) Warwick, University of. (Year, Month Day). *New study shows we work harder when we are happy.* Retrieved from https://warwick.ac.uk/newsandevents/pressreleases/new_study_shows/

55. O'Connell, B. (2019, March 23). *The Search for Meaning: Employees value salary, benefits and company leadership, but meaningful work drives job satisfaction more than ever.*

56. Wolf, J. (n.d.). *Bias: Definition, Examples, & Types. Berkeley Wellbeing.* Retrieved from https://www.berkeleywellbeing.com/bias.html

57. Bourke, J., & Dillon, B. (2018). *Diversity and Inclusion Revolution: Eight Powerful Truths.* Deloitte.

58. Lorenzo, R., & Reeves, M. (2018, January 30). *How and Where Diversity Drives Financial Performance. Harvard Business Review.*

59. Glassdoor Team. (2021, July 12*). What Job Seekers Really Think About Your Diversity and Inclusion Stats. Glassdoor.* https://www.glassdoor.com/blog/diversity-inclusion-stats/

60. Wongphaet, S. (2011). The 30 Years of the Samrong General Hospital. Bangkok: Giant Point.

61. *Lovichakorntikul, Petcharat, & Walsh, John. (2013). Dharma Teaching in a High-Tech Hospital Environment.*

62. *Kabat-Zinn, J. (2003). Mindfulness-Based Stress Reduction (MBSR). Constructivism in the Human Sciences, 8(2), 73-83.*

63. *Tang, Y.-Y., Tang, R., & Gross, J. J. (2019). Promoting Psychological Well-Being Through an Evidence-Based Mindfulness Training Program. Frontiers in Human Neuroscience, 13, 237. https://doi.org/10.3389/fnhum.2019.00237*

64. Khoury, B., Lecomte, T., Fortin, G., Masse, M., Therien, P., Bouchard, V., Chapleau, M. A., Paquin, K., & Hofmann, S. G. (2013). *Mindfulness-based therapy: A comprehensive meta-analysis.* Clinical Psychology Review, 33(6), 763-771.

65. Center for Compassion and Altruism Research and Education (CCARE). (n.d.). *8-Week Compassion Course.* Retrieved from https://ccare.stanford.edu/

66. Klimecki, O. M., Leiberg, S., Ricard, M., Singer, T., (2014). *Differential pattern of functional brain plasticity after compassion and empathy training. Social Cognitive and Affective Neuroscience, 9*(6), 873–879. https://doi.org/10.1093/scan/nst060

67. Kirby, J. N., Tellegen, C. L., & Steindl, S. R. (2017). *A Meta-Analysis of Compassion-Based Interventions: Current State of Knowledge and Future Directions. Behavior Therapy, 48*(9), 778–792.

68. Grant, A. M., & Schwartz, B. (2011). *Too Much of a Good Thing: The Challenge and Opportunity of the Inverted U. Perspectives on Psychological Science, 6*(1), 61-76. https://doi.org/10.1177/1745691610393523

69. Richardson, K., & Rothstein, H. (2008). *Effects of Occupational Stress Management Intervention Programs: A Meta-Analysis. Journal of Occupational Health Psychology, 13*(1), 69-93. https://doi.org/10.1037/1076-8998.13.1.69

70. Latham, G. P., & Locke, E. A. (2007). *New Developments in and Directions for Goal-Setting Research. European Psychologist, 12*(4), 290–300. DOI: 10.1027/1016-9040.12.4.290

71. Harkin, B., Webb, T., Chang, B., et al. (2016). *Does Monitoring Goal Progress Promote Goal Attainment? A Meta-Analysis of the Experimental Evidence. Psychological Bulletin, 142*(2), 198-229. https://doi.org/10.1037/bul0000025

72. Compassion Institute. (n.d.). *Compassion Cultivation Training (CCT) Program. Retrieved from* https://www.compassioninstitute.com/cct/#:~:text=As%20a%20graduate%2C%20you%20establish,contributions%20from%20our%20Founding%20Faculty.

73. Center for Values-Driven Leadership. *Benedictine University.* (n.d.). Retrieved from https://cvdl.ben.edu/

74. *Barrett Values Centre. (n.d.). Home. Retrieved from* https://www.valuescentre.com/

75. Greater Good Science Center. (n.d.). *Greater Good Science Center.* Retrieved from https://ggsc.berkeley.edu/

76. Huffington, A. (2016, November 30). *Welcome to Thrive Global.* Thrive Global.

77. Silsbee, D. (n.d.). *Doug Silsbee - Presence-Based Coaching.* Retrieved from https://presencebasedcoaching.com/doug-silsbee-legacy/doug-silsbee

78. *Everfi.* (n.d.). *Jeff Weiner's Compassion Project at UBS.* Retrieved fromhttps://everfi.com/blog/community-engagement/jeff-weiner-compassion-project-ubs/

79. Clifford, C. (2019, July 28). *Bill Gates took solo 'think weeks' in a cabin in the woods—why it's a great strategy.* CNBC. https://www.cnbc.com/2019/07/28/bill-gates-took-solo-think-weeks-in-a-cabin-in-the-woods.html

80. Nooyi, I. (2016, April 8). *Indra Nooyi on balancing career and family.* Fortune.https://fortune.com/2016/04/08/indra-nooyi-career-and-family/

81. Von Thiele Schwarz, U., & Hasson, H. (2011). *Employee self-rated productivity and objective organizational production levels: Effects of worksite health interventions involving reduced work hours and physical exercise. Journal of Occupational and Environmental Medicine, 53*(8), 838-844. doi:10.1097/JOM.0b013e31822589c2

82. Deloitte. (2021). *Well-being at the heart of the employee experience for the social enterprise.*

83. American Psychological Association. (2021, April). *The imperative of self-care. Monitor on Psychology, 52*(4). Retrieved from https://www.apa.org/monitor/2021/04/feature-imperative-self-care

84. Latham, G. (2004, November 1). *The Motivational Benefits of Goal-Setting.* Academy of Management Executive, 18. https://doi.org/10.5465/AME.2004.15268727

85. Grant, A. M., Nurmohamed, S., Ashford, S. J., & Dekas, K. (2011). *The performance implications of ambivalent initiative: The interplay of autonomous and controlled motivations. Organizational Behavior and Human Decision Processes,* 116(2), 241-251. https://doi.org/10.1016/j.obhdp.2011.03.004.

86. Linley, P. A., Nielsen, K. M., Wood, A. M., Gillett, R., & Biswas-Diener, R. (2010). *Using signature strengths in pursuit of goals: Effects on goal progress, need satisfaction, and well-being, and implications for coaching psychologists.* International Coaching Psychology Review, 5, 6–15.

87. a) Kizilcec, R., Piech, C., & Schneider, E. (2013). *Deconstructing disengagement: analyzing learner subpopulations in massive open online courses. In Proceedings of the Third International Conference on Learning Analytics and Knowledge* (pp. 170-179). New York, NY: ACM. http://dx.doi.org/10.1145/2460296.2460330

   b) Kearsley, G., & Shneiderman, B. (1998). *Engagement theory: A framework for technology-based teaching and learning. Educational Technology, 38*(5), 20-23. Retrieved from https://www.jstor.org/stable/44428478?seq=1#page_scan_tab_contents

88. Cooperrider, D. L., Whitney, D., & Stavros, J. M. (2008). *Appreciative Inquiry Handbook* (2nd ed.). Brunswick, OH: Crown Custom.

89. Halifax, J. (n.d.). *Meditation: Tonglen or Giving and Receiving: A Practice of Great Mercy. Cultivating Mercy.* Retrieved from https://www.upaya.org/dox/Tonglen.pdf

90. Yeshi, L. (2018). *Naikan-Based Compassion Training (NBCT) – A Theoretical Framework.* Master of Science in Positive Psychology Thesis. Life University.

91. Condon, P., & Makransky, J. (2020). *Sustainable Compassion Training: Integrating Meditation Theory With Psychological Science.* Frontiers in Psychology, 11, Article 2249. https://doi.org/10.3389/fpsyg.2020.02249

92. a) Jazaieri, H. (2018). *Compassionate education from preschool to graduate school: Bringing a culture of compassion into the classroom.* Journal of Research in Innovative Teaching & Learning, 1(1). https://doi.org/10.1108/JRIT-01-2018-0002

b) Jazaieri, H., Jinpa, G. T., McGonigal, K., Rosenberg, E. L., Finkelstein, J., Simon-Thomas, E., Cullen, M., Doty, J. R., Gross, J. J., & Goldin, P. R. (2012). *Enhancing Compassion: A Randomized Controlled Trial of a Compassion Cultivation Training Program.* Journal of Happiness Studies. DOI: 10.1007/s10902-012-9373-z

93. Krygier, J. R., Heathers, J. A., Shahrestani, S., Abbott, M., Gross, J. J., & Kemp, A. H. (2013). *Mindfulness meditation, well-being, and heart rate variability: A preliminary investigation into the impact of intensive Vipassana meditation.* International Journal of Psychophysiology, 89(3), 305–313. https://doi.org/10.1016/j.ijpsycho.2013.06.017

94. Ash, M., Harrison, T., Pinto, M. D., & DiClemente, R. (2021). *A model for cognitively-based compassion training: Theoretical underpinnings and proposed mechanisms.* Social Theory & Health, 19(1), 1-25. https://doi.org/10.1057/s41285-019-00124-x

95. Jazaieri, H., Jinpa, G. T., McGonigal, K., Rosenberg, E. L., Finkelstein, J., Simon-Thomas, E., ... et al. (2012). *Enhancing compassion: A randomized controlled trial of a compassion cultivation training program.* Journal of Happiness Studies, 14(4), 1113–1126. https://doi.org/10.1007/s10902-012-9373-z.

96. Jazaieri, H., McGonigal, K., Jinpa, T., et al. (2014). *A randomized controlled trial of compassion cultivation training: Effects on mindfulness, affect, and emotion regulation.* Motivation and Emotion, 38, 23–35. https://doi.org/10.1007/s11031-013-9368-z.

97. Weininger, R., Hatt, S. P., Shapiro, S., & Holden, A. N. (2017). *The Mindful Pause: Cultivating Emotional Balance through Mindfulness* (CEBtM). *J Yoga & Physio, 3*(4), 555616. https://doi.org/10.19080/JYP.2017.03.555616

98. Mantelou, A., & Karakasidou, E. (2017). *The Effectiveness of a Brief Self-Compassion Intervention Program on Self-Compassion, Positive and Negative Affect, and Life Satisfaction.* Psychology, 8, 590-610. https://doi.org/10.4236/psych.2017.84038

99. Gilbert, P. (2018). *Explorations into the nature and function of compassion. Current Opinion in Psychology, To Appear.* Centre for Compassion Research and Training, University of Derby, College of Health and Social Care Research Centre, Derby, UK.

100. Klimecki, O. M., Leiberg, S., Ricard, M., & Singer, T. (2014). *Differential pattern of functional brain plasticity after compassion and empathy training. Social cognitive and affective neuroscience, 9*(6), 873–879. https://doi.org/10.1093/scan/nst060

101. Kirby, J. N., Tellegen, C. L., & Steindl, S. R. (2017). *A Meta-Analysis of Compassion-Based Interventions: Current State of Knowledge and Future Directions. Behavior Therapy, 48*(10), 778–792. Elsevier.

102. Sprecher, S., & Fehr, B. (2005). *Compassionate love for close others and humanity. Journal of Social and Personal Relationships, 22*(5), 629–651. https://doi.org/10.1177/0265407505056439

103. Kwakyi, G. (Jul 28). *Eckhart Tolle teachings: What does Eckhart Tolle mean by "presence?"* The Musing Mind. https://www.gabekwakyi.com/essays/what-does-eckhart-tolle-mean-by-presence

104. Pāli Canon, the earliest Buddhist scriptures (Rhys Davids and Stede, 1921, *Pali-English Dictionary*)

    Various Buddhist scriptures, such as *the Dhammapada* and the *Sutta Nipata*

105. Dhammapada, a collection of Buddha's sayings (Muller, 2013, *The Dhammapada: The Sayings of Buddha*)

106. Watts, A. (1951). *The Wisdom of Insecurity: A Message for an Age of Anxiety.* Vintage.

107. Frankl, V. E. (1946). *Man's Search for Meaning.* Beacon Press.

108. Kabat-Zinn, J. (2005). *Coming to Our Senses: Healing Ourselves and the World Through Mindfulness.* Hachette Books.

109. Goyal, M., et al. (2014). *Meditation Programmes for Psychological Stress and Well-Being: A Systematic Review and Meta-Analysis Of Randomized Controlled Trials.* **JAMA Internal Medicine,** 174(3), 357-368.

110. Stellmach, S., et al. (2020). *AI in Coaching—Exploring Benefits and Challenges of AI-Enhanced Coaching—15th International Joint Conference on Computer Vision, Imaging and Computer Graphics Theory and Applications (VISIGRAPP).*

111. Kataria, G. (2019, November 5). *6 ways to leverage AI for hyper-personalized corporate learning. Better Up.*

112. Solanki, S. (2022, October 24). *Sentiment analysis using IBM Watson NLP: Understand the fundamentals of IBM Watson NLP and walk through the process of running and evaluating pretrained models to perform sentiment analysis.*